Pragmatic GXP Compliance

Pragmatic GXP Compliance

Successfully navigating the often complex and maddening world of regulatory inspections, inspection readiness, and knowing what's important

Eldon Henson

Dedication

This book is dedicated to all those individuals working hard every day to ensure that the healthcare products we use are safe and effective. To the operators committed to ensuring that the process is correct and everything is documented properly; to the laboratory analysts that strictly following analytical procedures; to the individuals weighing ingredients; to the analyst pulling samples of incoming materials; to the supplier auditor spending another week away from family auditing a new supplier; to the Quality Manager losing sleep agonizing over how to prepare for the next inspection... thank you! Your hard and meticulous work is why we can take our pharmaceutical products or use our medical devices with confidence.

Acknowledgments

I would like to thank everyone that played any role in the experiences, examples, and knowledge gained during my thousands of hours preparing for and hosting regulatory inspections in my decades in the industry.

Also, to all those public servants (e.g., regulatory investigators) that dedicate their lives to protecting the patient's safety through the enforcement of pragmatic GXP compliance... thank you.

Abbreviations and Acronyms

- Adulteration – Product that fails to meet any requirement of GXP regulations

- API – Active pharmaceutical ingredient – active ingredient or drug material used in pharmaceutical manufacturing

- CAPA – Corrective and preventive action – documented program for ensuring that unexpected or unusual events are identified, investigated, and corrected in such a manner as to prevent a recurrence

- CEO – Chief Executive Officer – typically, the top manager, thus, most responsible individual for ensuring GXP compliance with a firm

- Exception (or Excursion or Deviation) – An unexpected event occurring during the manufacturing or testing of regulated products that requires an investigation to determine the root cause and follow-up action to prevent a recurrence

- DEA – Drug Enforcement Agency – enforcement agency with the US responsible for managing controlled substances (e.g., opioids)

- Debarment – Legal prohibition for an individual to work in GXP-regulated industries

- FDA – US Food and Drug Administration – agency in the US responsible for the approval, control, monitoring, and management of all healthcare products (e.g., drugs, medical devices, foods, blood products, etc.)

- FD-483 form – Form used by the US FDA to document GXP violations observed during a regulatory inspection

- Fine – Monetary penalty incurred as a result of GXP violations

- FMEA – Failure Mode and Effects Analysis – a structured approach to discovering potential failures that may exist with the design of a product or process

- FOI – Freedom of Information – process for obtaining copies of certain documents possessed by US government authorities

- GMP – Good manufacturing practices – formal regulations which define processes, procedures, systems, and requirements for manufacturing government-regulated products

- GXP – General acronym describing any regulations mandated related to healthcare products (examples include GMP, GLP, GCP, etc.)

- Import alert – Detention of products without physical examination of imported products that appear to be misbranded or adulterated

- Injunction – A judicial order that restrains a person or company from continuing an action; typically, an injunction relation to GXP violations requires extensive restraint of operational freedom and significant costs

- IQ/OQ/PQ – Installation Qualification, Operational Qualification, Performance Qualification – series of validation protocols designed to verify that a system, operation, or equipment operates as designed and required

- OOS – Out-of-Specification result – typically, laboratory results that fail to meet pre-determined criteria and that require an investigation
- OSHA – Occupational Health and Safety Administration – US agency for ensuring health and safety of workers
- Recall – Removal of marketed product from distribution
- Seizure – Forced possession of products by a US regulatory agency
- SOP – Standard operation procedure – written procedure that outlines requirements and procedures for conducting certain activities

Contents

Pragmatic GXP Compliance

Successfully navigating the often complex and maddening world of regulatory inspections, inspection readiness, and knowing what's important

Part Four: The future of compliance and regulatory inspections

Introduction

The value of our work in quality and compliance

Back in 1982, perhaps the best thing that ever occurred in my career happened... my job was eliminated! I remember making that call to my pregnant wife to come pick me up from work. I was only four years into my career as a food industry research microbiologist and was now, suddenly, without a job. The news was devastating, but this single event made all the difference in my career. You see, that day began my journey into the pharmaceutical industry. Six months later, I started a new job as Microbiology Supervisor with a healthcare company that kept me involved in pharmaceutical manufacturing, quality, and compliance until I retired in 2016.

I believe working in the healthcare industry is the greatest place to be of all possible industry choices. Certainly, there are challenges that occur every day, but the ultimate payback is second to none. I believe that every day I was in the healthcare industry, I did something that made a difference in the life of some ultimate user or patient someplace in the world. So, what is the payback for all our work? How do we make a difference in the lives of our patients? Let me try to describe the fruits of our labors.

Most of us work in functions that involve compliance to GMP's, DEA regulations, OSHA requirements, and all their associated global regulations and laws. These regulations are often ambiguous and can seem to be onerous and less than value-added. I have often heard individuals question the value of correcting documentation errors with "a single line through with the new value recorded and initialed/dated." Others ask, "What is the value of doing three process validation lots to prove the process is in control?" We have probably all wondered whether we go too far with redundant steps, double-checks, % verification, inspection schemes, risk assessments, report re-writes, etc. Individuals not as close to this want to understand, "What is the value in all this extra work we call quality or compliance?"

Value is one of those popular terms used in business circles these days. Everyone wants to know the value of our latest acquisition, the value provided by a consulting arrangement, the value we expect from a significant Capital investment, the value drivers for a particular initiative. Understanding "value" is important for us to ensure that our direction is correct and that our priorities are properly placed. Value is synonymous with "return on investment" or "payback". When someone asks about value, they are really asking, "When and what will be the payback for this?" So, it follows that many want to know, "What is the payback for all of these GXP activities? When will our extra effort to qualify that equipment, document that activity, repeat that step, or marry the science-with-the-regulations in a way that allows us to release that batch?"

Well, I would like to share my thoughts on "when we'll see payback for all our efforts in quality and compliance":

- We get a payback during an FDA inspection when the investigator asks to review 10,000 documents and we have confidence that every page of every document will be done right, documented well, and properly tell our story of quality and compliance

- We get a payback every week when our complaint reports, representing literally millions of doses of products distributed, show only minor issues with product shipped to patients – it is gratifying knowing that the products our patients receive are right, safe, and will fulfill the mission and life-changing impact intended

- We get a payback every month when we see improvement in those critical quality metrics that define how we're doing

- We get a payback when someone asks where we work and we can tell them proudly – often, that same individual will tell of a relative or friend that works or has worked for us or their own story of using our products

- We get a payback every night when we walk to our car knowing that we did our best work to make a difference in the lives of others

- We get a payback when we encounter someone like Sammy, a little 5-year old boy I know that struggled with cancer for three years knowing that we might play a small role in Sammy's life and recovery

If you will take the time to consider all we do and why we do it, you'll easily see that quality and compliance have a payback. What we do makes a difference!

That is one of the reasons I have written and assembled the information you have in your hands. I spent 35 years of my life dealing with GXP compliance. I have probably been directly involved in over 100 regulatory inspections in my life, perhaps half of these as the direct agent-in-charge. I spent countless thousands of hours developing systems, processes, and procedures for complying with GXP requirements. I understand what it takes to be successful in the area of GXP compliance.

This is not a typical "GXP Compliance" book. I will not attempt to talk about the nuts-and-bolts of process validation protocols, cleaning validation, or training. My goals with this book are as follows:

1. *Education* - To help compliance practitioners teach others the importance of GXP compliance and create an enhanced culture of compliance

2. *Focus* - To provide focus on GXP compliance activities that are important and, thus, stop doing activities that provide no GXP compliance value

3. *Readiness* - To provide guidance on compliance and inspection readiness activities that focus on the "majors" and minimize activities that are meaningless

4. *Outcomes* - To provide tools and advice that enhance success of regulatory inspections and management of inspection outcomes

5. *Future* - To provide perspectives and guidance on the future of regulatory inspections and activities that need to begin now

In short, my intent is to inject pragmatism into the complex web of GXP requirements and offer help navigating toward a more successful outcome. The temptation regarding GXP compliance is to comply plus... go above and beyond... just in case! However, this approach is cumbersome, expensive, and frustrating.

You will also find a listing of recommendations at the end of the last chapter. This list can be used to summarize the content of this book or it may serve as an aid to you in identifying additional steps you can take to enhance compliance in your own operation.

So, let's dive in and explore what we do, why we do it, how we can focus on the most important, and prepare our organization for the best possible inspection outcomes as we move forward.

Part One

Why does GXP compliance matter (other than the obvious, of course)?

1

Quality and Compliance Matter

Quality

Quality can be defined in several ways:

- For a product or item, it means conformance to specifications, fitness for use, or attaining the level of performance required
- For a person, it means a level of satisfaction, contentment, enjoyment, pleasure, fulfillment, or meaning
- For an activity, it means that it is something attainable, provides value, but could have a cost associated with it

So, summed up, we might define quality as that level of fitness that provides a satisfying, enjoyable, or meaningful experience. When we carve up this concept, there are five key elements of Quality that could be called "critical factors." Let's look at each:

1. **Attainment of a standard or expectation** – Any definition of quality must include some element of calibration against a standard or some level of user expectation. One product is deemed a quality product when compared to another. One car is

deemed quality because of its performance history compared to other cars. An individual is deemed a quality person when their life is judged against others or when the individual simply deems it so. A product has achieved a level of quality because it conforms to specifications or is deemed fit for its intended use. So, quality is always an attribute that is relative to other similar products, activities, or persons.

2. **Provides meaningful intrinsic value** – Anything of quality provides value to the user, recipient, or observer. Often, that value is not something tangible, but is intrinsic. Another way of expressing this is to say that quality brings pleasure or satisfaction that might not be measurable, but is experienced, nonetheless. For example, a quality life might not be measurable, but is certainly felt and experienced by the person and those around him/her.

3. **Provides a satisfactory or pleasurable experience** – When I think of something of quality, I always get a positive or satisfying sensation. For example, when you think of a "quality" song, book, vacation, product, person, or experience, don't you almost feel a smile bubbling up inside you? Who can't smile when you think of a "quality" piece of pie with a scoop of ice cream on the side? Quality is a positive, satisfying, or pleasurable attribute that we should seek in everything we do, buy, or experience.

4. **Is attainable with a specified level of effort** –The definition of quality should include a requirement that it be attainable, though with some effort exerted. Quality can be cheap and easy (e.g.,

beautiful sunset, laughter of a child, or holding hands with your spouse), but it may include a cost (e.g., training to run a marathon that you complete, learning and using a second language for the first time, achieving your lifetime best score in golf, etc.) worth paying.

5. **Provides a benefit greater than the associated cost** – Philip Crosby once wrote a book called *Quality is Free.* In it, he states that the value provided by top quality always offsets the price paid to achieve it. By spending the time, cost, or effort to achieve something of quality, we always get a payback. Certainly, there is a limit to this in the business world – no buyer of generics products will pay more to get high-gloss graphic photos on the carton that will be thrown away, for example. However, in most cases in business and in our personal lives, striving for and attaining something of quality is worth the cost and sacrifice paid to achieve it.

In healthcare businesses, Quality of products, service, or the combination of the two often differentiates what we consider "top quality" from all the rest. In our personal lives, the quality of our life is never measured purely in the material success we attain, but by our family, our friends, and by the impact we have in the lives of others.

Compliance

Compliance is the act of conforming, acquiescing, or yielding. It is the willing conformance or obedience to the requests, requirements, or expectations of others. In the world of GXP's, compliance means to adhere to both the letter and spirit of the law.

You will notice that the definition of compliance does NOT say to do more than is expected, to do it faster than required, or to do it better than others. Yet, we all know that continuous improvement is an expectation of all global regulatory agencies. How many times have you seen or heard the terms "industry standards" or "agency expectations"? In healthcare industries, compliance can better be defined as:

Compliance is the act of willing adhering to the written letter, spirit, and ongoing, increasing expectations of regulatory agencies as measured by applicable laws, statutes, guidance documents, and industry standards as they evolve, grow, and mature.

Our ability and willingness to comply with GXP requirements often determine our reputation, business success, ability to grow, and, ultimately, the safety and well-being of our final customers or patients.

Compliance to GXP requirements is the capstone to our business. Without compliance, we have no healthcare industry. However, let's look closer at what GXP compliance is not. GXP is NOT:

1. ***Doing more than is expected*** – There is nothing in GXP's that requires that we go above and beyond laws and expectations. Though some may believe that failing to continue the leapfrog approach (e.g., continuing to do more that industry peers to demonstrate a commitment to compliance), it is not required.

2. ***Acting faster than required*** – Certainly, when we find ourselves deficient in complying with GXP requirements, speed is critical. But, GXP compliance does not mean that you are compelled to inflict unreasonable timelines to advance processes and systems beyond what is reasonable when you are currently operating in a state of compliance.

3. ***Performing better than others*** – Regulatory agencies began inappropriately using comparative information to measure GXP compliance in the 1980's. At that time, investigators began measuring "commitment to compliance" by ascertaining how one firm compared to another rather than simply determining whether currently observe processes and practices met requirements outlined in regulations. This practice continues today leading to some to believe that compliance is a form of competition. It is not and we must not let that belief drive our compliance activities.

Regardless of the evolution of GXP requirements and our definitions, quality and compliance are essential in the healthcare industry. Compliance is often ambiguous, frustrating, and challenging. Educating others, especially those new to our industry, is an ongoing effort. We are often impatient when compliance trumps science. The pace of change can be snail-like. Interpretation of requirements leads to disagreement and irritation. Nonetheless, we work in the best industry the world has ever created. Our work, of which compliance to GXP requirements is essential, makes a difference to so many. What we do may mean the difference between life and death to someone we love. That is why we do what we do and why all this effort, and the sweat and tears that go along with it, matters.

2

The relationship of company culture to compliance culture

There has been much talk lately in the business world about "culture" – what it is and how to improve it. Some companies make use of culture surveys or engagement surveys to measure the current company culture. Then, they develop action plans to improve the culture believing that a better culture drives better performance, thus, better business results. So, this begs the questions, "What defines culture and is it really possible to improve it? And, if you do, what improved results can we expect, especially for GXP compliance?"

Culture can be defined as "the way of life, especially the general customs and beliefs, of a particular group of people at a particular time."

> *"Culture is not what you say it is. Culture is what you do."*
> *– Jennifer Ledet*

I believe in this 100%! We do not change a culture with slogans, banners, songs, and campaigns. We create and/or change our culture day-by-day, action-by-action. Culture is our way of life in the specific function, group, floor, plant, or company in which we reside. It is what we do and, though a targeted campaign might gradually influence what we do, the true culture is largely determine by the leaders of that group.

"The culture of any organization is shaped by the worst behavior the leader is willing to tolerate." - Steve Gruenter and Todd Whitaker

Everyone is a leader. You lead something – a function, a group, a line, a family, a team – each person is responsible for other individuals to some extent. What kind of "culture" are you creating in that group? If you believe the quote by Gruenter and Whitaker above, you create a culture by what behavior you tolerate. For example, in a family, the culture is defined by how much discipline you expect from each member. Do you require that everyone make their own bed each day? Do you require that everyone put away their own things? The culture, then, is determine by whether you allow one member to consistently violate the rules of behavior.

In a company, the culture is, to a large extent, defined by how we allow employees to treat each other; by what standards of behavior we require; by the level of personal accountability we demand; by the level of quality we deem our minimum standard; and by how much personal flexibility we allow. It is possible to define a company culture by requiring that everyone dress the same, by requiring everyone to work 12 hours/day, by prohibiting anything deemed fun, or by demeaning individuals when they fail to attain perfection. We can also define a company culture by allowing individuals to take reasonable risks, by encouraging individual innovation, by demanding that we treat each other fairly, and by providing an environment that encourages work/life balance. You can see that our actions as leaders define what culture our group will have. In other words, we define the "way of life" for our team or family.

So, how do we use this concept to create a culture of compliance? How do we instill in the organization the belief that compliance is required? If we believe that the culture is defined by the behavior we encourage and what we tolerate, there are three key factors that will determine the level of compliance:

1. *Commitment to compliance displayed by senior management* - Certainly, it is easy to talk about being committed to compliance. Senior management at every healthcare company will talk about the strong commitment and dedication to quality and compliance. But you know their words truly represents the values of the company when you see:

   - Capital and budgetary funding dedicated to systems, processes, facilities, and people to embrace and improve quality/compliance performance

   - Quality/compliance reporting to the CEO of the company (or at least to the next level down) - this helps ensure that these functions have a direct line of communication to and from the CEO

   - Top management consistently requesting updates on compliance/quality initiatives and, likewise, speaking of performance to shareholders, customers, and employees

   - Clear acceptance of quality/compliance performance responsibility and accountability by senior management

2. *Actions taken by management when things go wrong* - It is easy to be "committed to quality/compliance" when things are going well. Senior management will tout their amazing organization when new products are approved or when inspections go well. However, you can learn much about the company culture when you observe management actions when things go wrong. For example:

   - What is the senior management reaction when a recall is required? Is there a tendency early in these discussions to identify "who allowed this to happen"?

   - Does senior management tend to focus on "the end justifies the means" when discussing difficult product disposition decisions? Is there pressure to "make this problem go away"?

   - Are most difficult quality/compliance discussions more focused on blame than they are on learning from the problem?

3. *Attention given to "doing the little things right" from the top to the bottom of the organization* - Finally, perhaps the best measure of the compliance culture of an organization is to look at discipline. I recall hosting a European Union regulatory inspection at a facility. On the first day, the investigator asked to walk through and look at the men's locker room. He even asked to look in a few lockers. Later, I asked him why he felt this was an important inspection activity, he responded, "I

always learn a lot about an organization when I inspect their locker rooms. If I observe that employees take pride in that area and typically have neat and organized lockers, I know that this pride will transfer to their work when they manufacture pharmaceutical products. If they do the little things right, I know they will be attentive to the bigger things." When an organization drives excellence in all things, the culture is more likely to perform well with the details of GXP compliance.

I would argue that the best way to enhance the culture within our group/team/company is to embrace the statement above by Gruenter and Whitaker... we must stop allowing behavior that does not represent what we desire for our group. All of us can help to create the culture we desire. We each have a part in creating a culture of encouragement, fair treatment of others, high standards of work, and fun. When we consistently demonstrate that compliance is a value that we will never compromise, our level of quality and compliance will grow.

3

Educating Management: How much adulteration is too much?

How many of you have heard something like the following from management?

- *What's the problem? All we're talking about is a few specks in the tablets.*

- *What do you mean we can't release that batch? It met all the finished product specifications, didn't it?*

- *Can't we just retest that batch to see if it is really OK?*

- *How much adulteration is too much? (Note: Yes, I really did hear a member of management ask me that one time.)*

Granted, comments like these should be rare in the 21st century. Nonetheless, helping management, especially when their background is in a non-scientific area, understand the basic elements and requirements of GXP's is an ongoing challenge.

So, what is the proper approach for helping management, especially senior management, understand the important role they have in ensuring compliance with GXP requirements? Before we look at some specific approaches, let's begin by reviewing management responsibilities in a GXP environment, the benefits of creating a strong compliance culture, and the enforcement options at the hands of regulatory agencies in the event we fail to maintain the necessary level of compliance.

Responsibilities of Management

What is it exactly that management must do to ensure an appropriate level of compliance? To understand how to best educate management about their responsibilities for GXP, it is best to review those responsibilities.

When operating properly in a GXP environment, management will:

1. ***Create a mission, vision, and Corporate Quality Policy geared to GXP compliance*** - Perhaps, the most important responsibility for management is to create the overriding messaging of the importance of quality compliance. This is most often established through a mission statement and/or vision statement that clearly articulates the corporate commitment. Such a statement does a couple of things: it continuously reminds employees, stakeholders, and customers that quality compliance is important AND it ensures accountability. When your mission/vision statement declares a commitment to compliance, it makes it much more difficult organizationally to cut corners. A strong compliance commitment included in a mission or vision statement partnering with a Corporate Quality Policy works to establish that quality compliance is a value that cannot be compromised.

2. ***Establish a Quality Unit with the proper
    organizational reporting structure*** - Of course,
    words are cheap. Saying that quality compliance is a
    value without demonstrating it through solid
    actions renders it meaningless. GXP's require that
    complying firms establish a Quality Unit with
    adequate organizational strength to ensure
    compliance. In short, unless the Quality Unit has
    the ability to stop production or reject
    noncomplying products, its organizational strength
    is inadequate. In fact, GXP's require that the Quality
    Unit be given status equivalent to functions such as
    Production, Engineering, and Supply Chain. Quality
    must sit at the table at which decisions are made
    that potentially impact quality or GXP compliance.
    Failing to create such a structure is a management
    failure that has severely impacted other firms (see
    Regulatory Agency Enforcement Options below).

3. ***Create a Quality Unit with adequate credentials,
    numbers, and organizational support to execute
    GXP compliance*** - In addition to creating a Quality
    Unit with adequate organizational strength,
    management must ensure that members of the Unit
    have adequate training, experience, and skills to
    perform all GXP activities. This typically means that
    Quality Unit leaders have demonstrated ability
    leading their respective functions. It also means
    that management adequately fund the Unit. By this
    I mean enough resources are provided to perform
    all required activities. It is very tempting to focus
    resources on activities that "produce revenue" and
    view quality compliance personnel as overhead. I
    would argue that a properly resourced Quality Unit
    can often "pay for itself" by ensuring an ongoing

supply of conforming, high quality products. Failing to resource quality functions adequately is a common root cause for firms cited for non-compliance issues.

4. *Create a periodic management review process that ensures management knowledge and oversight of Quality data and compliance performance* - GXP's require that management have a process in place to ensure awareness of quality compliance through a systematic review of quality performance data. Many firms conduct this formal data review on a monthly or quarterly basis. This review should be adequate to ensure that management is aware of potential adverse trends, quality compliance risks, and actual performance of products at the consumer level. This GXP requirement is one of the elements of the legal basis for "management is without excuse" (discussed below).

5. *Establish a visible and vocal quality compliance posture* - Many GXP regulated firms establish a strong mission or vision statement accompanied by a Quality Policy, then never discuss quality compliance again. Management must make quality compliance an ongoing discussion point. For example, quality compliance should be a topic in town hall meetings, be a typical topic in company newsletters, receive significant discussion in annual corporate reports, and Quality Unit leaders should be routinely highlighted in forums with senior management. Company leaders should mention quality compliance performance in public venues. All of these combine to demonstrate clearly that

quality and compliance are more than talking points, but values the help define the success of the company. In short, management must make clear that no year is a good year in which quality or compliance issues resulted in significant regulatory agency or consumer impact.

6. ***Ensure ongoing commitment by recognizing and rewarding strong quality compliance performance*** - Companies are usually quick to highlight strong performance of sales and marketing organizations. Most firms have an "annual sales meeting" in which top performers are recognized and rewarded. However, do individuals involved in achieving significant achievements in the quality compliance arena similarly recognized and rewarded? A failure to do so often seems to relegate these individuals to second tier status when it comes to company success. Management must demonstrate the importance of quality compliance by recognizing and rewarding it.

7. ***Establish systems to manage performance to ensure compliance*** - A basic responsibility of management is to manage performance. This also applies to GXP compliance. Creating goals and objectives that measure the output of the Quality Unit and associated contributors to GXP compliance (e.g., Production, Engineering, and Supply Chain) is critical to ensuring that needed ongoing level of performance in these areas.

8. ***Establish an organizational structure and process for escalating known and potential quality compliance issues*** - Management must be involved in key decisions impacting quality compliance.

Establishing such a process for escalating these issues is a responsibility often left to informal communication. Management of firms that give lip service to quality compliance will often work to abdicate their responsibility to be aware and involved in key decisions. I have even heard of firms that adjust their organizational structure to delegate these responsibilities to others. For example, I heard of one firm that had the Quality Unit reporting to the Legal Department, essentially allowing other senior management the shield of the Legal Department to deflect their responsibilities for quality compliance. Senior management at firms that are committed to quality compliance seek opportunities to be directly involved, not create ways to avoid it.

9. ***Establish a process for identifying risks for non-compliance through audits, assessments, and data review outside the periodic management review process*** – Members of management at some firms are afraid of bad news. However, committed management will seek ongoing input into the performance of these quality compliance systems. Establishing robust internal audit programs, assessments of system performance (e.g., Supplier Quality performance), and ongoing review of performance data are signs of management committed to GXP compliance. I know one firm that formerly had their GXP Compliance Internal Audit function reporting directly to the CEO. This provided an ongoing, direct line of communication to the top manager of the company for potential risks. Later, this same company altered that organizational structure under a new CEO and

eventually agreed to a consent decree and large fine to remedy ongoing GXP compliance issues. This organizational change may not have been directly involved, but I cannot imagine a significant slip in GXP compliance when the CEO was getting routine feedback on GXP performance from the leader of the Corporate Compliance function.

10. ***Provide adequate resources and commitment to facilitate continuous improvement of systems, equipment, facilities, and personnel performance*** – In addition to the Quality Unit, it is a significant management responsibility to properly fund other continuous improvement initiatives. For example, new equipment, updated facilities, and enhanced personnel skills must be funded. You cannot establish solid systems and expect them to remain current without ongoing enhancement. I am aware of a firm that once had a facility so modern and advanced that US FDA personnel routinely visited the facility for training to see "how it should be done." However, that firm failed to maintain and continuously improvement the operation and a few years later it was the source of a Warning Letter alleging poor maintenance and inadequate resourcing to perform basic GXP responsibilities.

Benefits of a Strong Compliance Culture

Aside from avoiding the negative consequences associated with inadequate compliance, there are other benefits to a strong compliance culture.

First, there is an element of ***organizational discipline*** needed for compliance. The mere fact that a strong compliance approach means that you have written procedures, trained employees, maintained equipment, and standards against which to measure performance... all key attributes of many successful operations. When your entire organization has the needed discipline to properly fulfill GXP requirements, success in other areas of the business is likely.

GXP requirements also include, as a built-in, critical element, systems for identifying and correcting problems. In effect, GXP's drive toward ***continuous improvement***. In a strong GXP environment, there is an ongoing culture of correcting issues, making the operation better, and preventing events that could negatively impact the business or product quality.

As we might expect, a strong culture of GXP compliance should result in ***better product quality***. When processes are consistent, employees knowledgeable and disciplined, and practices in place to ensure that high manufacturing standards are achieved, we can be sure that we will experience fewer rejections, less product loss, and higher conforming finished product.

Finally, when we achieve a strong culture of compliance, the ***consumer or patient impact*** will be better. GXPs, by definition, exists to ensure the safety, purity, identity, strength, quality, and efficacy of distributed product. Thus, we should expect that the ultimate patient experience is higher when compliance is better.

Regulatory Agency Enforcement Options

Regulatory agencies have been given significant power to enforce GXP compliance. This is true globally. Reviewing these enforcement options with management can help inspire a greater respect for compliance.

Many of the "tools" used by regulators are well established and well known. For example, most individuals in this industry understand the significance of US FDA 483 items and their global equivalents. Likewise, the use of import alerts, recalls, debarments, seizures, injunctions, and fines are also well established.

There are a couple of enforcement options, though, that are valuable to review with management when discussing the need for enhanced GXP compliance. One example comes from the Danish Medicines Agency (DKMA) which suggested to Europharma DK ApS (a repackaging firm) that the firms needs a new CEO that will appropriately deal with compliance concerns. Apparently, repeated citations of GXP deficiencies did not elicit an adequate response, so DKMA used its influence to drive accountability to the top manager in the company. It has become increasingly common for regulatory agencies to publicly communicate that senior management bears the burden for compliance.

In the US, the "Park Doctrine" has been in use for several years to ensure that top management cannot abdicate responsibility for compliance. The Park Doctrine stemmed from a court decision that declared that management responsibility did not require "awareness of wrongdoing" to be considered liable for GXP deficiencies. In effect, any individual in the company that "is in a position in a corporation with responsibility and authority to prevent or promptly correct" a GXP problem could be held individually responsible for the violative acts. Thus, individual company officers (e.g., CEO, President, Senior Vice-President, etc.) have been prosecuted successfully with fines and imprisonment imposed.

So, management must understand that they cannot abdicate any responsibility for GXP compliance to others down the line in the company. Regulatory agencies now view members of top management as the responsible party for all activities relating to GXP compliance. Helping management understand this is an important step in their "education" about GXP compliance.

Approaches for Educating Senior Management

From a practical standpoint, we are now at that point where we answer the question, "What steps can we take to educate our management about their important role and responsibility in ensuring a strong GXP compliance culture?" I believe there are 4 key steps that can help management to become fully knowledgeable and supportive of these efforts:

1. ***Review with them the management responsibilities, benefits of compliance, and regulatory agency enforcement options discussed above*** – Certainly, some individuals in senior management roles, especially those new to GXP regulated operations, do not have the experience to fully grasp the challenges and responsibilities included in their roles. For these

individuals, it is imperative that they be exposed in detail to these elements. Helping them to understand their personal and individual responsibility may alone be enough to elicit full and active support. For example, a newly named CEO with a background only in Sales or Marketing is suddenly given responsibility for all operational functions, may feel that expending resources for activities "behind the scenes" is less valuable to the overall firm than spending on more visible sales or marketing initiatives. However, when they realize that, like others, they could be prosecuted for a failure to ensure GXP compliance regardless of whether they were personally aware of concerns, they tend to become much more active in learning and understanding how they can avoid compliance issues. However, senior managers do not often become full supporters of GXP initiatives simply out of fear. Thus, there is more to their education needed.

2. ***Highlight the competitive landscape regarding GXP compliance posture*** - Most members of senior management are highly competitive. They continuously seek competitive intelligence to learn what their peers are doing and how they must react to remain in the game. Taking advantage of their competitive nature can be beneficial with GXP compliance, as well. Help management understand what actions peer companies are taking regarding compliance activities. For example, if a peer company is implementing a new software system that will provide more rapid and accurate data trending information, share that information. If a peer company has received a 483 citation for failing

to properly resource GXP-required functions, use that to help justify your needs in similar situations. By using information of competitors, especially in what is considered your company peer group, you can often educate management on the need to support initiatives that strengthen compliance.

3. ***Demonstrate the "value" of compliance*** – GXP practitioners should never avoid talking about the value of compliance to the company. In fact, speaking in "dollar terms" is often the best way to help others in management understand the need. In fact, if you cannot justify any expenditure in terms of value, it is probably not needed. I believe there are three areas of value that need to be re-enforced with management:

   a. *Cost of non-compliance* – Most of us are familiar with the term "cost of poor quality." This is useful for demonstrating overall loss for poor performance relating to product costs. However, a similar calculation is useful for demonstrating the value of a strong compliance operation. When you total all costs for non-compliance, the number can be substantial. These costs would include costs for: recalls, investigations, complaints, follow-up auditing, batch rejections for GXP failures, CAPA actions, etc. Calculate all costs associated with a failure to execute GXP compliance perfectly. This number will undoubtedly be larger than you expect and can be helpful to demonstrate the importance of a strong compliance culture.

b. *Direct financial impact* – Many individuals underestimate the direct financial value of a strong compliance operation. Consider the value of improved product release times on inventory costs, production planning, and product supply. If you could eliminate all time associated with retesting, investigations, and compliance failures, what would the direct impact be? Or, what would be the value to a faster new product approval time? For example, if you anticipate that a new product will generate $365 Million in annual sales, each day that final approval is delayed costs you $1 Million in sales.... Per day! With that in mind, how important is it to have a pre-approval inspection occur without compliance issues? How important is the entire effort to produce a "first-time right" submission package? Determine the direct value of perfect compliance and utilize that information to educate senior management.

c. *Indirect financial impact* – There is an opportunity impact for strong compliance. For some products, the potential market is impacted by your compliance position. The ability to do business is often strongly influenced for active pharmaceutical ingredient (API) suppliers by their current and future potential compliance position. The value of business opportunities cannot be overlooked as an element of the value of GXP compliance.

4. *Enforce the importance of "internal" and "external" reputation regarding GXP compliance* – Finally, the impact of GXP compliance position on employees (internal), patients (external), and stakeholders (external) should not be ignored. Because so many companies have had business impacts due to poor compliance, it has now become an important recruitment tool. When you can portray a solid and respected GXP compliance position, it does help recruitment and retention of top talent. There is also certainly an impact to shareholders for the same reason. Finding a way to emphasize the fact that a company in GXP regulated industries must be considered a reliable and trusted compliance partner is another important educational tool for management.

Helping management understand the important role and responsibility of leading a GXP regulated company is a key factor to the success of that firm. Using the approaches outlined can facilitate that key educational process and instill quality compliance as a value that will not be compromised.

4

Enhancing compliance in a cost-conscious environment

Current GXP compliance environment

We find ourselves today in an interesting GXP compliance environment:

- US FDA claims that they are more dedicated than ever to science, yet enforcement remains strict adherence to written GXP's whether or not current scientific principles render some GXP elements obsolete

- Regulatory agencies monitor and work diligently to guard against drug shortages, yet they continue to demand strict GXP compliance in areas that are the direct cause of those same shortages

- "Science and speed" are touted as the new way of approaching compliance, yet agencies remain tethered to outmoded requirements for pre-approval of seemingly minor changes

- Regulatory agencies understand the need for cost improvement to ensure both survival of firms and continuity of supply, yet they continue to maintain that cost containment is no excuse for GXP compliance excursions

Certainly, the basic tenant of product safety has never altered, however, finding the balance between fundamental GXP compliance and productivity/cost/survival for many healthcare companies is an everyday challenge.

So, what approaches are acceptable for the healthcare firm struggling to control costs, yet step-up to the ever-increasing (rightly so, I might add) requirements for ensuring product safety and manufacturing integrity articulated in GXP's? Let's take a closer look at the challenges we face and some strategies you might use to help achieve that balance.

Regulatory agency views on cost cutting

The pharmaceutical industry was king when I first began working in healthcare. Those were the best of times in many ways. I recall interviewing at a company in the early 1980's. This company has by now undergone several rounds of acquisition and consolidation, so its name no longer exists. But, this company's campus was beautiful! There were dozens of gardeners to tend the professionally designed and manicured grounds. The buildings were immaculately maintained. There was a private dining hall with a full-time chef to serve the senior management team. A private jet was always available and ready for travel to outlying plants, customers, or suppliers.

In the "old days", pharmaceutical companies had products providing a significant margin with no end in sight. The product pipeline was full and life was good. There was no need to be concerned with product costs or margins that other industries, such as consumer products, had to face. In effect, pharmaceutical companies were fat and happy and reaping the fruits of great products with little competition, cost pressure, or shareholder scrutiny since many of these giants of their time were privately held.

Eventually, times changed. Consolidation in the industry occurred. New pressures to continuously satisfy the insatiable demands of shareholders for these newly public companies mounted. New foreign competition entered the scene. So, over the span of 2 or 3 decades, the pharmaceutical industry began facing the same cost pressures that other industries had faced for years.

In the face of these new cost pressures, healthcare companies began using the same "cost management" techniques perfected in other industries, such as downsizing, restructuring, and redundancies. For the first time, cost cutting became the norm in healthcare industries.

At the same time, regulatory agencies were enhancing compliance enforcement activities. Agencies began using terminology, such as "The Quality Control Unit failed to fulfill its regulatory requirements...." Regulators were driving hard toward ensuring that the Quality Units were, in fact, ensuring that all GXP requirements were being met, not merely serving as test and release entities.

Additionally, regulatory agencies (mostly FDA) began holding senior management more responsible for GXP compliance. A number of large, successful firms were forced to court and signed consent decrees that cost millions of dollars in fines and forced strict new requirements, such as the use of third party GXP experts to review and approve operational activities. I remember, in particular, the fine of $100 Million levied against Abbott Laboratories in 1999 for repeated compliance issues in its manufacturing facilities. In essence, at the same time that cost cutting pressures were hitting, FDA enforcement pressure was increasing.

So, how do we balance the need to remain cost effective, yet attain a high compliance level? What can we do to continuously improve within the confines of strict regulatory requirements and cost pressures? Following are seven proven strategies for managing GXP operations in a cost-conscious environment. Let's take a look at each and determine how they might apply to your operations.

Strategies for managing a cost-conscious environment

1. ***Identify and prioritize "untouchables"*** – Face it… there are many items that should be considered "untouchable" when discussions about cost cutting are concerned. To ensure that these items remain intact, it is important early to articulate what these are and communicate a renewed commitment for compliance to the entire organization. Some examples include:

   - *Clearly written GXP requirements* – No question, items clearly articulated in GXPs must be fulfilled. By this, I mean expectations that pose no options. For example, GXPs state that employees be trained to perform their specific GXP job functions. This is unalterable. However, it does not say exactly how that training is to be accomplished. So, looking at alternatives for training should be considered, but elimination of training must remain.

- *Recent commitments to regulatory agencies* – Another untouchable category should be any commitment recently made to a regulatory agency, either in response to an inspection or other agency correspondence (e.g., Field Alert Report). Though these commitments may not be clearly articulated in GXP's, a commitment to a regulatory agency must be held to the highest level of expectation. For example, if you commit to engineering modifications to your sterility suite to prevent environmental failures in a response to a FD-483 form, you can expect that this will be reviewed during the next inspection. A failure to follow through with this commitment will certainly result in further regulatory enforcement. You must not fall short of these commitments without discussion and negotiation with the appropriate agency.

- *Regulatory agency expectations for standard practices* – Requirements outlined in Guidance Documents, Inspection Protocols, or as articulated by similar manufacturers as "best practices" are also considered GXP requirements by regulatory agencies. Be cautious delving into these "gray areas" when considering cost cutting measures.

- *Commitments made in filed manufacturing or testing processes or procedures* – Another area that must be carved out as sacred is what has been committed in filed processes. Certainly, these should be under strict change control mandates, but some areas might provide some flexibility that would be discussed during cost improvement conversations. Be certain that everyone involved understands the need to remain vigilant regarding controlled systems for considering, making, and validating changes.

- *Practices that protect the health or safety of employees* – Though not necessarily GXP requirements, Quality and Compliance practitioners must always be supportive of efforts to protect employees.

2. ***Re-examine prior compliance enhancement commitments*** – As mentioned earlier, recent commitments to regulatory agencies must be considered in the same untouchable category as explicit GXP requirements. However, I have seen many examples of commitments made years earlier that no longer apply and should be reconsidered. For example, I once questioned the need for a report being prepared monthly that summarized environmental trends. The report required the retrieval of data from an automated tracking system and was distributed to a number of functions as a 20+ page hard-copy document. This report was developed despite having a very robust electronic tracking system that generated trending reports, alarms for trend excursions, and detailed information available with a few computer clicks. The hard-copy report was not used by anyone. However, the group responsible for the report responded, "We committed to FDA that we

would create and distribute this report, so we have to continue doing it." The truth is, that commitment was made over 10 years prior to that and preceded the automated computer tracking system now in place. Common sense must prevail. Simply continuing to do something because someone, somewhere made a commitment is not value-added. These activities are ripe for elimination.

3. ***Use risk management methodologies for identifying compliance improvement opportunities*** – For cost reduction opportunities that fall outside the "untouchables" list, a good starting point is to utilize risk management methodologies to identify possibilities. Utilizing an analysis tool (such as FMEA) is an excellent approach for identifying high-priority cost improvement targets. In the final analysis, though, you must consider overall value for making the changes targeted. Considerations must include, of course, the value of the change in monetary terms. Identifying the annual savings is important, but you must also consider what you give up. For example, what is the cost to implement the changes contemplated? Are the cost reductions sustainable or one-time? Will the change be perceived as an abdication of responsibilities? Will the change result in additional investigations, new reporting, or additional oversight? Someone once said that there is a difference between price and cost. In the case of cost reductions in a GXP environment, this may be more true than for any other situation. You don't want to reduce immediate, short-term costs, yet, in the longer

term, cost yourself significantly more because of unexpected issues arising later.

4. ***Maximize use of data trending rather than react to individual excursions*** – I often recall the first time I was part of a facility that implemented in-line total organic carbon (TOC) monitoring. This system was a continuous system for monitoring the relative water quality. The system provided continuous data and provided alarms when limits were exceeded. After we validated the system, we placed the system into use with a limit of 500 ppb of TOC. What we didn't realize was that, as is the case with most systems, the TOC can vary throughout the day depending upon the conditions or activities occurring at the time, such as cleaning, heavy water usage, etc. So, during the first few days of use, we had TOC spikes above the 500 ppb limit numerous times. Because this was our limit, each excursion required a deviation and investigation. What we soon learned was that continuous TOC monitoring is an excellent tool for monitoring the performance of the water purification system but is not necessarily instantaneously useful for gauging the water quality at that instant. Thus, we had to implement more generic limits that did a better job of monitoring system performance. By doing so, we continued ensuring a high-quality water source AND we avoided unnecessary excursions and investigations each time the TOC spiked above 500 ppb.

When you are seeking ways to eliminate costs, utilize the systems and data you are already generating to provide more value-added information. Rather than reacting to every excursion of a non-critical parameter, revise your data monitoring processes to utilize data as trend information rather than as discrete data points. A good example of this might be routine environmental monitoring (EM) data. Certainly, EM data for the sterility suite must be treated as discrete points requiring individual action (class 100 or grade A or ISO 5). However, in a class 100,000 area (grade D or ISO 8), is it really critical to execute isolate identification and an investigation for each discrete excursion? For less critical areas, could you use trend data to gauge cleaning efficacy, the need for system redesign, as a monitor for employee performance, or other longer-term purpose? The use of Contamination Recovery Rate (CRR), as described in detail in USP <1116> may be one approach that can be used to enhance the use of EM trending data to alleviate the requirement to react to every individual limit excursion. I know of one firm that generates literally hundreds of deviation investigations annually that could be eliminated simply by a more robust use of trend data for their less critical controlled area monitoring.

5. *Major on the "majors"* – When considering continuous improvement approaches, the model most often emulated is the Toyota Manufacturing System. Toyota mastered the concept of "kaizen" or many small improvements add up to significant improvements. This approach is proven to bring significant, long-lasting improvements. However, in a drive to improve costs and save resources,

patience is often in short supply. In these cases, there is a tendency to "reduce costs by 10% within 90 days" or some other similar goal. So, how can we ensure GXP compliance, yet support significant, rapid cost containment? For the GXP practitioner, it is imperative that we focus our attention on enhancements that can reduce costs quickly. That often leaves out improvements that require prior regulatory approval or changes that require extensive validation. Some of these may be necessary, but you are unlikely to drive significant cost reductions quickly by focusing on these activities. So, what recommendations would I provide in this situation? Let's look at eight examples of areas that should represent your "major on the majors" way of thinking. You will note that these eight areas represent the 8 Types of Waste typically considered in Lean Manufacturing concepts, but they can also apply to compliance activities:

- *Defects* (Rework, wasted materials, or repair) – Material waste is likely one of the greatest impacts to product costs in most manufacturing operations. We drive these costs down relentlessly, yet they remain higher than desired. Look for ways to reduce these losses, such as:

    - ✓ Reduced numbers of samples taken for in-process, finished product, or stability samples

    - ✓ Reduced stability test points

 ✓ Optimization of fill levels using
   tightened process capability

 ✓ Use of technology to reduce flush
   volumes during changeovers

- *Processing* (Unnecessary steps or activities
  that add no value) – Eliminating non-value
  added activities should be an ongoing
  effort, especially during a cost reduction
  initiative. The use of a risk management
  tool may provide the best objective way to
  identify opportunities. Examples might
  include:

   ✓ Reduced testing using validated
     Certificates of Analysis for raw
     materials

   ✓ Incorporation of information
     recorded on forms into the Master
     Batch Record

   ✓ Eliminate reviews and approvals for
     low risk activities

   ✓ Review frequencies and intervals for
     internal and external audits

- *Overproduction* (Too much, too soon) –
  Production planning often requires an
  extended planning horizon because of
  finished product release times. A review of
  opportunities to reduce these planning
  times can frequently result in more optimal

production cycles. Opportunities to improve release times might include:

- ✓ Altering laboratory work shifts to ensure 24/7 testing capabilities

- ✓ Improved laboratory cycle times might facilitate the financial justification of critical new testing equipment

- ✓ Rapid, technological solutions to bottlenecks

- ✓ Improved availability of data reviewers or dedicated individuals to conduct critical investigations

- *Waiting* (Wasted time waiting for the next step of the operation) – In my experience, significant time is spent in production waiting for samples to be tested, data reviewed, and results released. By reducing waiting times, the improved efficiency may result in significant cost improvements, especially in "sold out" operations. Examples might include:

  - ✓ Shifting testing from lab to at-line along with dedicated testing resources

  - ✓ Shifting from low- to high-technology approaches, such as UPLC from HPLC

✓ Transferring responsibility for some in-process tests from "QC" individuals to Production individuals (requires training, verification, and monitoring)

- *Motion* (Unnecessary movement of people) – By using industrial engineering tools to assess people movement, you can often eliminate unnecessary movement, thus, reducing labor, time, or material loss. Examples of potential efforts might include:

  ✓ Shifting laboratory testing equipment and people closer to production areas when sample movement to the laboratory is required

  ✓ Shifting manual data/information input to electronic systems

  ✓ Eliminating unneeded reports

  ✓ Shift some meetings from in-person to online, thus, reduce time from a typical hour meeting to half that time

- *Transport* (Unnecessary movement of materials) – When needed materials are closer to the point of use, unnecessary movement can be eliminated or shifted to other more valuable tasks. Consider:

  ✓ Moving material storage closer to production areas. For example, is it better for label storage and control areas to be closer to the warehouse, where it typically resides, or to the production areas where labeling materials are used?

✓ Whether there is value in always salvaging excess materials remaining at the end of production back to inventory – in some cases, the cost of tracking, moving, reconciling, and returning materials to stock are more than the actual value of materials

- *Inventory* (Excess parts or materials) – Several inventory optimization activities have already been discussed (reduced laboratory cycle times, optimized fill levels, etc.). Other opportunities might include:

    ✓ Faster disposition of returned, rejected, or nonconforming materials

    ✓ Faster completion and disposition of validation batches

    ✓ Temporary shifting of personnel to ensure 24/7 final batch disposition capabilities

- *Underutilized human resources* (Not using skills and abilities of people to fullest potential) – Much waste occurs because we fail to delegate reasonable activities to the lowest capable level of the organization possible. Examples include:

✓ Allowing lower levels of the organization to execute final approvals of protocols, reports, and procedures

✓ Requiring fewer approvals for similar documents (Note: I have seen some reports or procedures in organizations that require 10 or more approvals for the document to be considered approved. Most of these individuals provide only cursory review... or none at all!)

✓ Routinely delegate authority for tasks to capable and trained individuals

✓ Assign specialists to critical bottleneck areas to facilitate faster and better responsiveness for key decisions (such as Regulatory Affairs personnel to manufacturing sites)

6. *Redeployment strategies* – One of the ways to experience rapid cost reductions is to redeploy existing personnel to other more critical activities. Care must be exercised when this occurs to ensure that personnel requirements are balanced with individual capabilities and training. However, when done correctly, shifting personnel can bring significant improvements both short- and long-term. Factors that must be considered for such redeployment situations include:

● *Retention of focus on high priority areas or high benefit projects* – Do not take your eyes off the most important balls! There are some you simply cannot drop, thus, reducing resources in these areas must be resisted. I recall a situation in my past in which some desired to redeploy individuals assigned to an important LIMS project to the bench to alleviate product backorder issues. On the surface, this appeared to be one means to provide short-term relief for a customer service issue. However, the LIMS project was so important to ongoing compliance issues and productivity opportunities that it made no sense to redeploy these personnel. By the time these individuals were retrained and reacclimated to their laboratory responsibilities, the crisis would have passed. Avoid the temptation to take away resources from critical activities merely to place a band-aid on problems that should have been remedied previously.

- *Continuous assessment of risks* – If you do choose to redeploy resources from one function to another during a cost reduction initiative, you must monitor the potential for introducing new compliance risks. You are not ahead when you simply shift one kind of compliance risk with another. If you can smoothly make these changes (e.g., moving analytical resources from raw material testing to finished product testing, for example), do so if it makes sense. But, you must constantly ensure that these "temporary" changes do not introduce new problems.

- *Employee impact* – The impact of redeployment of personnel on the affected employees cannot be underestimated. Regardless of the circumstances, you should not make such changes without consultation with affected employees. Their buy-in and positive participation will determine whether the effort is successful. You should consider:

  ✓ Childcare or other personal impacts, especially if work hours or shift changes are contemplated

  ✓ Training, skills, and familiarity with the proposed new duties

  ✓ Impact on salary, bonuses, objectives, or potential or expected promotional opportunities (e.g., career impact)

  ✓ Solicitation of other potential solutions that will provide the same or better result with more favorable impact on employees

  ✓ Impact on retained employees when other employees are furloughed, or positions are eliminated

- *Bench strength development* – There are times when redeployment of employee resources provides strong long-term benefits. For instance, when employees are shifted to new or different responsibilities, they add to their skillsets. As you enhance the types and varieties of skills, you are essentially strengthening your available bench strength. On the other hand, it is often tempting in redeployment situations to return the person that "used to do that job" back to a function to facilitate a temporary need. When this occurs, you risk disenchanting that employee or delayed his or her development to assume new or greater responsibilities.

- *External resources* – There are also times when actually adding external resources may provide long-term cost improvement. Though seemingly contradictory, the external resources may provide the ability to eliminate a backlog of work, implement new productivity projects, or reduce wastes that, in turn, allows a lower cost operation thereafter.

- *Zero base employee analysis* – The use of zero base budgeting is a well known technique for constructing a budget without prior biases (supposedly). This same approach can be used for developing a resource budget. This approach is conducted basically by answering several questions:

✓ What "must do" activities must be accomplished and in what amount of time?

✓ How many skilled labor hours are required to accomplish those tasks (include all away from work hours)?

✓ What other "should do" or "hope to do" tasks would be included?

✓ What is the labor requirement for these other tasks?

✓ What tasks are we currently doing that do NOT fall into the category of "must do" or "should do" or "hope to do" that can be eliminated?

✓ What is the total labor requirement (include needed skills and experience) required to fulfill all key activities for this function?

✓ What is the gap between our zero based assessment and our current actual resource pool? This number represents the cost reduction opportunity.

- *Short- or long-term* – Any employee redeployment opportunity must consider whether the arrangement will be short- or long-term. The reality of the situation must be well communicated to affected employees and others and all possible efforts must be undertaken to fulfill commitments made to employees. This is critical to develop and maintain credibility during times of difficulty.

7. **Stop short-term thinking** – Perhaps, the greatest detriment to successfully balancing a cost reduction initiative with improved compliance is short-term thinking. In other words, knee-jerk reactions often result in increased costs or reduced quality. This short-term thinking must be eliminated to achieve success as you work to navigate the difficulties of this balance. Let's look at a few examples:

   - Eliminating gang-testing of laboratory samples to prioritize that "red hot" batch we need before the end of the month

   - Assuming that the way we have always done it is the way we must continue doing it

   - Believing that we cannot negotiate with regulatory agencies to apply new approaches that make sense scientifically and economically

   - Accepting defeat simply because we believe the effort is too hard, too long, or too risky to achieve something amazing

   - Capitulating to cost reduction initiatives handed down by management without considering alternatives or the impact on compliance

I am reminded of a saying that typifies the short-term thinking that we must work to eliminate:

"We're going to save money no matter what it costs!"

In a cost cutting environment, we must remind ourselves daily of the need to ensure that the actions we take are reasonable and do not invoke detrimental effects in other areas of the business.

8. ***Employee engagement/involvement is important*** – Times when severe cost reduction initiatives are ongoing are stressful times. The impact on employees can be physical (lack of sleep, fatigue, or more prevalent illnesses), emotional (lack of motivation, depression, and uncertainty), and personal (concerns with childcare, financial demands, or an unknown future). Thus, it is imperative that you engage employees as early as possible and as much as possible in the process. Some of the benefits of employee involvement could include:

   - Better overall results, better ideas, or better implementation plans

   - Alternatives that can enhance desired results

   - More motivated workforce that can achieve a more efficient implementation of needed changes

   - Less risk regarding employee concerns, compliance risks, or product quality impact

- Greater buy-in throughout the organization

- Faster realization of cost reduction initiatives

- Improved sustainability of results

- Lessened perception that compliance and product safety will be impacted

Because cost reduction is so often associated with poorer compliance/quality, it is imperative that efforts be transparent, negotiable, and flexible. If such critical efforts occur without the involvement of those individuals most critical to implementation, you should not/cannot expect success that will yield the cost reductions desired nor will they maintain the high level of compliance expected.

Finally, to illustrate our approach to cost cutting in a period of increasing compliance enforcement, let's look at the following three items:

- FAST
- GOOD
- CHEAP

The old paradigm around these three items is "Pick two – you can have two of the three, but not all three." The theory is that you can have fast and good but expect to pay for it. Or, you can have good and cheap, but don't expect it on your timetable. Or, you can have fast and cheap, but the quality will be poor.

I contend that we must adopt a new paradigm around these three items. I believe that we CAN have all three. We can have fast, good, and cheap (or lower cost) simultaneously, but there is one caveat. We can't have all three by doing things the way we have always done them. To have all three, we must be willing to do things differently. We must think outside the box. We must involve others in the process. We must spend Capital to implement new technology. We must train employees in new things in new ways. We must approach compliance from a new perspective. Indeed, we can have it all, but we must be willing to go places in ways that are, perhaps, uncomfortable or unfamiliar.

5

When relentless becomes reckless

Successful individuals are often described as "relentless" in their pursuit of victory, completion of a difficult task, or dedication to an effort. I have historically viewed a relentless person as one that has strong positive character traits, but I think it is possible to take relentlessness too far. The dictionary definition of relentlessness is "...unyieldingly severe, strict, merciless, rigid, or harsh." So, is relentlessness good or can it be harmful? When does relentless become reckless, especially in the context of GXP compliance? Let's explore this...

I have had the occasion to watch hummingbirds visit a feeder at my home. Last year was a banner year for hummingbirds judging by their numbers. Anyway, our feeder has four slots where birds can hover and drink a sugary liquid. They can also visit flowers nearby. I would term the hummingbirds as relentless in their pursuit of food. They spend nearly all day coming to the feeder or flowers and seem to have few other interests. They have some rests from these efforts, but they are few and they don't last long. Perhaps, hummingbirds must be relentless in order to survive. Despite this, hummingbirds exhibit a sense of caution. When feeding, they are constantly alert for danger and quickly flee when spooked.

There are also humans that have this same sense of "relentlessness" in their pursuits. Some think of their work or career pursuits 24/7. I recently heard of one CEO of a start-up company that intentionally sent texts or email messages to applicants at odd hours (such as 9pm on a Saturday night or 11am on a Sunday morning) to test their responsiveness. If they failed to respond within three hours, they "did not fit the culture" desired by the CEO. When relentlessness goes too far, it becomes an obsession or an addiction... it becomes reckless. And, when that occurs, the individual's life gets out-of-balance.

Similarly, the pursuit of "perfection" in GXP compliance activities can shift from relentless to reckless. For example, senior management, especially those from disciplines outside science or technology, cannot comprehend why a manufacturing site cannot achieve perfect GXP compliance. After all, the requirements are written, in existence now for over 40 years, and in place globally for all healthcare companies. So, why is it that the percentage of regulatory inspections with no citations is probably less than 50%? Label control requirements have changed little since GMPs were first issued in the 1970's, yet packaging/labeling issues have comprised one of the top 3 reasons for product recalls for each of the last 10 years?

I have worked in more than one firm or environment in which the strong expectation was all FDA inspections would result in zero FDA-483 form observations. And, because of this "requirement", the tendency is to overreact and perform activities that cost too much, add unnecessary complexity, or compromise other more important activities.

So, is "relentlessness" a good or bad trait? I think, like so many other things, anything we do to the extent that it harms other areas of our life is bad. When we pursue our career to the detriment of our family, we have gone too far and recklessly endanger our relationships. Going too far is missing most of the key life events of our children, neglecting our spouse, or failing to nurture other relationships. Going too far to attain an arbitrary compliance goal, especially when observations are often subject to personal whims and preferences of the investigator, is excessive.

However, being relentless (or undeterred) in continuously enhancing overall compliance or completing a specific task is probably a good thing. For example, if you have a critical assignment that must be completed on schedule, it pays to be relentless in completing the task on time. Creating a continuous improvement culture that says, "We are never satisfied with our level of compliance" is a solid management objective.

There are other examples of relentlessness that are admirable. Most of us have heard of or know individuals that have suffered a severe health crisis yet were relentless to overcome the adversity they experienced. So, in many ways, being relentless to accomplish a specific task is a good thing. However, being described as a relentless person (that is, one that pursues something "in an unyieldingly severe, strict, merciless, rigid, or harsh" manner) with no regard for balance is a negative thing.

Here are a few character attributes that we should strive to exhibit in our lives that communicate in the same way as relentlessness:

- Persistent – ability to stick to a task until it is completed, even in the face of failure

- Diligent – can be relied upon to complete assignments in a high-quality manner

- Reliable – true to their word

- Dedicated – committed

- Focused – aligned with the target at hand

We should pursue "appropriate and timely" relentlessness. We should also be aware that even the hummingbird takes a break. Relentlessness must be used only for important tasks or efforts. It is difficult to sustain indefinitely.

Crossing the line of relentlessness to recklessness is a small step. When we do, we become:

- Careless – sloppy, ignoring appropriate risk

- Thoughtless – lost focus on the target or goal

- Impetuous – petty, wasting time on unimportant tasks

- Impulsive – jumping to conclusions; irrational

- Irresponsible – failing to fulfill basic responsibilities

- Foolhardy – making unforced errors

Bottom line… we should be relentless to accomplish needed tasks when they are important, meaningful, and impactful to ourselves or others, such as GXP compliance. However, exercise the caution of the hummingbird… be alert. Don't cross the line from relentless to reckless.

Part Two

Not everything we do under the umbrella of "GXP Compliance" is really required (or even necessary)

6

Dispelling GXP Myths

This is an active time in the healthcare regulatory compliance world. Many new initiatives from regulatory agencies are underway at a time when industry is working to balance compliance with cost control, drug shortages, consolidation, unique world events, and new technology. As a result, there are some that might feel that FDA (and other global regulatory entities) might be relaxing or allowing more flexibility in their enforcement efforts. I would like to look at several of these notions or myths that might prevent us from thoroughly and completely fulfilling our duties to comply with current requirements. Here are just a few of these GXP myths and what we need to do to keep from falling into the trap of nonchalance:

Myth #1: The end justifies the means

Certainly, in this day and age, GXP practitioners do not believe that we can violate specific GXP requirements, provided the final product meets specifications. However, there are subtleties that can crop up. For example, the thought that as long as we document a GXP discrepancy, complete an investigation, and get QA approval, we can overcome any manufacturing issue is false! Regulatory investigators have every right to ask us how these GXP discrepancies impact our validation for that product/process, what impact it might have on our filed process, or evaluate any additional validation we might have conducted to ensure the discrepancy had no adverse impact. In short, we cannot assume that a thorough and complete investigation report is enough to justify excursions from approved processes.

Myth #2: Regulatory agencies do not connect the dots

In companies with multiple locations and some product portfolio complexities, it is tempting to think that our response to GXP compliance can be limited to each locality. In other words, if we comply in our location, we don't have to worry about what happens at other sites. Not true! Regulators have become more sophisticated regarding "global" compliance. They now have increased ability to monitor issues to determine if we have company-wide systemic issues. They cross-check performance issues at one location with similar issues at other locations. Many US FDA Warning Letters in recent years reference compliance concerns at multiple issues. Sites receiving inspections are often asked about approaches to compliance concerns noted at other sites in the same company. I have colleagues at companies that are frequently challenged for issues at other firms or sites. Global GXP enhancement is now now considered a "current" compliance expectation.

Myth #3: Relationships and trust don't really matter to regulatory investigators

Regulatory agencies are in the business of protecting the consuming public. Safety is the bottom line. So, when dealing with manufacturers, Investigators have a limited time to assess operations to answer the question, "Is the firm complying with GXP to the extent that has been inspected and do I have confidence that they comply in areas I have not inspected?" Thus, in addition to assessing what and how we do what we do, they also try to determine whether they can trust our employees to do the right thing. If they feel they can trust us to do the right thing, it enhances the confidence they have in us and what we do. I was once at a company that the FDA District Compliance Director said, "Because I know you as individuals and trust that you will address these issues, we will not pursue a Warning Letter." In other words, the trust they had developed through our relationship allowed them some discretion in the compliance action they took. So, relationships and trust in people do matter!

Myth #4: We can hide our problems from regulatory investigators

Investigators are somewhat predictable. We tend to learn, over time, what they will examine, how much time they will spend, and what activities will not receive attention. However, investigators become more sophisticated and more data-driven, we can be sure that they will find our vulnerabilities. In addition, the laws and regulations have changed over recent years to allow investigators access to more of our operations than ever before. They now have access to nearly everything we do. So, we cannot assume any more that dirty laundry will remain hidden.

Myth #5: Our strong record of compliance will cover us in the future

Though relationships are important, we can no longer rely heavily on a track record of compliance. Yes, a history of compliance is possibly the greatest predictor of future inspection success. But, agency investigators have demonstrated in the past few years that they will hit hard, when needed, regardless of your reputation or history.

Several firms have recently experienced their first compliance issues in years, showing that agencies are willing to look at each inspectional result as a fresh, single data point.

Myth #6: Regulatory investigators will never look at developmental data or early studies

In the US, FDA now has greater regulatory power to examine data than ever before. And, now, they appear to view developmental data in the context of potential data integrity concerns. They have shown that, in order to verify regulatory submission data, they will go back much further to evaluate early data. Thus, we must be even more rigorous to ensure that all developmental data, including for early studies, is well documented and inspection ready.

Myth #7: Regulatory agencies care more about science than compliance

Despite frequent speeches touting regulatory agency interest in science-based compliance, they still default to the details of regulatory compliance. In other words, science will not trump compliance for nearly any compliance/inspection situation. So, we cannot feel that a solid scientific argument will overcome a clear regulatory non-compliance. Some international agencies, however, are more open to applying a solid scientific rationale in the field during inspections. I would not expect it, though, on a regular basis.

Myth #8: Electronic data are completely trustworthy

There is a tendency to think, "As long as our data are generated and archived electronically, regulatory investigators will accept it and have no compliance

concerns." Wrong! A very high percentage of Warning
Letters and compliance concerns recently have cited issues
with data integrity of electronic systems. We simply cannot
make assumptions about the integrity of electronic data
short of executing a comprehensive compliance plan.

Myth #9: If we don't know about a problem, regulatory investigators will give us a pass

Ignorance is not excuse for non-compliance with GXPs. In
fact, even senior management is liable for GXP issues
whether or not they have been informed directly of the
issue. Therefore, we must all ensure that we know the
regulations, we know whether we have gaps, and that we
have plans and actions in place to remediate those gaps.

Myth #10: Regulatory investigators do not care about product costs or cost of poor quality

This one might be a bit tricky. Investigators do NOT care
about what is costs to comply with GXP regulations. We
cannot say that it costs too much to do what is needed to
produce safe and effective products. However, they are
interested in cost of poor quality in that it can often be an
indicator of poor systems or poor execution. If they find
that our cost of poor quality is higher than they see at
other firms, they may dig deeper to determine why.
Regulators are also concerned about ensuring a
continuous supply of medically necessary products. If we
pose a risk of causing a supply shortage that could impact
patients, regulatory agencies are very concerned. In fact, in
the US, we must communicate to FDA when there is a
possibility of a drug shortage. So, in effect, FDA is
concerned about product costs to the extent that we must
maintain an adequate supply to patients that depend upon
our products.

So, hopefully, a review of these myths may help those of you dealing with GXP compliance every day and give you something new to consider as you work to balance company needs, patient requirements, and regulatory compliance.

7

Non-value added, feel-good GXP activities that do nothing to advance compliance

If you are like me, you may have been frustrated from time-to-time expending significant resources to accomplish something that you know will not improve compliance or product quality. Yet, you continue doing it, you continue hiring individuals to do it, and you continue feeling as though you could be spending your time and money much more effectively elsewhere.

On top of this, regulated industries have been under increasing pressure to control costs, eliminate waste, and enhance efficiency. Is it even possible to eliminate some of these seemingly "untouchable" non-value added GXP activities?

I would like to list a few of my pet-peeve GXP activities and suggest possible alternatives that might add more value. I'm sure each of us in this industry could add activities to this list, but I will cover only 6 that come to my mind:

1. *25-Page SOPs* – It is time to eliminate the notion that it is more important to include every possible detail in a Standard Operating Procedure (SOP) than creating a document that individuals will actually

use to do the job. Certainly, you need to fulfill the need to have detailed procedures to ensure operators cannot *ad lib.* But, in the course of fulfilling normal duties, it is expecting too much to believe that operators will read the SOP line-by-line each time an action is performed when the SOP is dozens of pages. Instead, it is far better to consider one of these alternatives:

- Break long SOPs into shorter, more simple procedures

- Create simple work instructions that include only the details needed by operators to accomplish necessary tasks

- Include imperative requirements in batch records with associated documentation of critical steps

- Create graphical representation of steps that can be referenced at the workstation or that can be used with computers, tablets, or smart phones

Perhaps the best alternative is to incorporate these details into an electronic batch record system. These systems include mandated compliance of critical steps and eliminate much of the tendency to ignore SOP requirements (or at least their review or use) during the actual manufacturing process. However, these systems are expensive and time consuming to implement.

2. ***Read and sign training documentation*** – Does anyone still believe today that asking someone to "read" and provide a signature/date is adequate training to ensure adequate understanding of

documentation requirements? I have seen situations in which an employee will read/sign 50 SOPs in one day to document that they were "trained" on the procedure. Then, the firm will proudly present that it has a thorough and comprehensive training program knowing that these signatures do not represent comprehension or competence. Even a shift to require a quiz to demonstrate competency is not necessarily proof that the individual has the understanding today or, better yet, a year from now, to do the job properly or correctly. Possible alternatives include:

- Shifting the focus from read/sign to more comprehensive use of the written procedure when the action is performed. It is more important to use the procedure today than to attempt to recall what you read months ago.

- Use of presenter-led training to ensure that key elements of procedures are articulated and understood. In many cases, helping individuals understand the "why" for a requirement will promote better compliance than simply reading that an action is required.

- Shift to a master/apprentice training relationship. This will ensure that the "apprentice" is trained one-on-one by someone that is an expert on the procedure or activity.

- A combination of all of these suggested approaches. Relying simply on one approach is not likely to be an approach best suited to every individual.

3. *Boilerplate IQ/OQ/PQ documentation* - Somewhere along the line, I think we fooled ourselves into thinking that if we have enough pages in our IQ/OQ/PQ documents and do it every time, we have fulfilled the original intent of equipment or process validation. I have seen numerous examples of using standard protocol documentation to the extent that critical factors are forgotten or omitted. I believe taking the time to think through and apply good science is better than simply generating protocols that offer no value.

4. *Ignoring science simply because no action was required*- Speaking of science... I frequently see examples where good science is ignored because there was no specification or requirement to document or explain events. We can become so focused on the requirements that we stop being a scientist. Using our training and experience is needed.... and, it is expected by global regulators.

5. *Retraining as a corrective and preventive action (CAPA) response* - When retraining is our primary response to an event, my first response is that you didn't truly identify the root cause. Overusing retraining as our default response offers no value and will only lead to a recurrence. Be more thorough to ascertain the real "why". Then, apply actions that have a greater opportunity to remedy the failure.

6. *Reacting to every environmental excursion in low risk areas*- Most firms with aseptic operations struggle with environmental failures. Reacting with due diligence is necessary for failures or excursions in critical, high-risk areas. However, continuing to conduct an investigation and react to every

individual excursion in low risk areas is not adding value. It is better to formulate a system that uses these data as a monitor of how well the overall system is performing (e.g., cleaning, operator competence, training, engineering systems, etc.). Finding a way to monitor, but not overreact is needed. One question to ask is, "Is our facility/system designed to prevent every potential excursion in low-risk areas? If not, how can I extract meaning from individual results? Should I use individual results in a controlled manner (e.g., control charting) versus reacting to each individual excursion?"

Avoiding these non-value-added activities can free up resources to focus on more urgent compliance and product quality issues. Don't be afraid to think outside-the-box to improve your operations. Don't keep doing these activities simply because you have always done them. Apply good science to enhance what you do and how you do it. We can no longer afford to waste critical resources on these activities that do nothing to enhance compliance or product quality.

8

Dear healthcare company: Do these things really benefit the patient?

At this stage in my life and health, I think I can speak very competently about being a patient or end user of your pharmaceutical or medical device products. I have had multiple surgeries, take daily pharmaceutical products, have metal medical devices in my knee and back, sleep with your products, and, in short, am an experienced user of your products. In addition, I worked in your industry for nearly 40 years, so I have that perspective, as well.

Today, I want to talk about things that REALLY matter to patients (used synonymously with end user). I know that many healthcare companies talk about their commitment to patients being first and foremost. In fact, one large, old, established company has this first line in their corporate values statement:

"We believe our first responsibility is to the patients, doctors and nurses, to mothers and fathers and all others who use our products and services."

However, do you really take this seriously? When you are creating your mission statement, crafting goals and objectives, and training your employees, is your first and primary focus really on patients?

I think I am speaking for many/most/all patients when I urge you to consider anew your true first priority. When you are contemplating key business decisions, do you really include patients as a key stakeholder before shareholders, the community, or employees? Do you believe that if you take care of your patients, every other aspect of your business will take care of itself?

Many healthcare companies have been criticized in recent months in the media for exorbitant pricing, supply problems, excessive executive salaries, inappropriate influence of physicians, and the pursuit of profits above all else. Most of these criticisms would have been tempered if those same companies were diligent in ensuring that the value of their products to the patient was unquestioned. When your products have unquestioned value, benefit, and quality, many of these other criticisms can be dispelled.

Let me discuss a few things to consider before you answer this question. I want to list a few activities that patients DO NOT CARE that you do. These things mean NOTHING to us when we are talking about our health, our lifestyle, and our ability to live a full and meaningful life. When a patient is in pain, all they really care about is getting relief. Certainly, we understand that you need to have satisfied, engaged, and involved employees. Of course, we understand that you are in business to make a profit. By all means, you have a responsibility to the communities in which you operate. Yes, we agree that you need to ensure that every employee has equal opportunities without barriers caused by direct or systemic biases. However, we believe that some of you have drifted from your commitment to the patient. In your zeal to be all things to all people, you have forgotten your core purpose. Have you made an effort to tie these things (each of which has merits) to the patient experience? Let's look at the "things that mean nothing" list, then I will talk about things that really DO matter to us.

Things you do that patients <u>do not</u> care that you do
(keep in mind that these are just examples – there are probably other things you do, when carefully considered, could be added to this *list)*

1. *Political activism* - Many of you seem to spend more time advocating for a political view or candidate than you do advocating for patients. We have political action committees, but do any of you have a "patient action committee"?

2. *Diversity and inclusion programs* - Yes, we understand the intent with these programs. However, have you taken the time to determine if the value of these efforts in money and resources yields any benefit to patients? We appreciate your concern and effort on behalf of unmet needs, but please ensure that these efforts (which, for most of you, includes the staffing of entire departments and corporate structure) are yielding value that includes benefits for patients. From a patient perspective, we don't care who you hire, as long as it is the best person for that particular job function. Just find a way to hire the best people, keep them motivated, treat them with respect and fairness, and help them facilitate value and quality in the products we use. These programs do have value, please just ensure

that the benefits to the organization also flow to the patient.

3. *Employee engagement activities* – Again, we understand the arguments FOR these programs... happy employees are more productive, more innovative, and yield better results. However, when do you go too far? When do go so far trying to engage employees that you forget to engage patients?

4. *Sustainability* – Most of you, by now, have very active sustainability programs (e.g., green, recycle, reduced carbon footprint, etc.). We applaud the intent. However, when it comes to relieving pain, curing disease, or improving our lifestyle, we don't really care. Do what you can in the area of sustainability, but please ensure that these efforts enhance, not detract from the overall patient experience or impact.

5. *Non-value-added packaging* – We don't need packaging with 7-color glossy print. Honestly, we throw out the packaging immediately after receiving our products. This is an area that you should work to differentiate yourself from others with value, not "bells and whistles" that do nothing, but add cost.

6. *Corporate branding and marketing* – How many healthcare firms change their corporate branding each year? And, when they do, how many $millions are spent doing so. Sure, this may matter to other stakeholders (such as shareholders, investors, and industry watchdogs), but it does nothing to improve our experience.

There are many things you do that we truly do value and appreciate. Let's look at a few of these (some of you should transfer some of your spending from activities listed above to these areas).

Things that really <u>do matter</u> to patients

1. *Cost control* - Finding ways to improve the cost for us is always appreciated. We do understand the need to recoup your R&D investments and turn a reasonable profit. However, it is always just as important to ensure that everything you do provides value and will ultimately benefit your primary stakeholders, especially the patient.

2. *Innovation* - We appreciate your efforts toward continuous improvement. We appreciate pharmaceuticals that can be taken orally rather than injection only. We appreciate the ability to spend less time in the hospital. We appreciate less invasive procedures. Innovation that improves the patient experience is always appreciated.

3. *Employee development* – We understand the need to help your employees stay current, stay motivated, and continue making positive improvements to your products. Efforts spend to advance the capabilities of your valued employees ultimately will benefit us.

4. *Customer service* - The availability of needed products and having individuals that can answer our questions is important. When you enhance the interface between company and patient, our experience is improved.

5. ***Product quality*** – We expect your products to be of high quality and to do for us what you promise. Please ensure that you remain diligent in these areas. When cost cutting is needed, please look elsewhere before you jeopardize the quality of your products.

6. ***Business continuity/compliance*** – Because we count on you and your products, your efforts to remain in business and viable are important. We have read too many accounts of products that had to be recalled or market shortages simply because companies failed to remain diligent or compliant. Efforts in these areas are important for us.

Please understand that the intent of this message is simple... it is important to occasionally ask the question, "If patients are important to our business, will this activity/program/project/objective provide a benefit to the patient. If not, is it really that important to do? Would our patients pay more because we do this?"

9

An FDA-483 observation is not necessarily the worst thing that can happen

Firms conducting healthcare business in the US always use the FD-483 form as the standard or benchmark regarding GXP compliance. The general impression or assumption is that you are in GXP compliance if you do not receive a 483 observation for a particular area or function. But, is this true? Is it possible that the lack of a 483 observation does NOT necessarily mean you are compliant? Is it possible that you could receive a 483 observation and yet be in substantial compliance? In the next few pages, we'll look at a number of typical questions regarding FD-483 forms, their observations, and what they mean with the goal of helping you better understand your own compliance status. Also, please keep in mind that, though the US FDA utilizes the FD-483 form to address potential compliance concerns during inspections, all other regulatory inspectorates utilizes some form of report that lists observed deviations from GXP standards based on the investigator's review. When I mention 483 observation or form, please assume it equally applies to systems used by these non-US inspectorates.

What is the FD-483 form? What does it mean to the FDA in terms of GXP compliance?

The FD-483 is the form number used by FDA investigators to record their observations regarding violations of current GXP requirements. The form is prepared and presented at the conclusion of an inspection. Non-US regulatory inspectorates will typically provide a similar written list of concerns, or at least a verbal list, when they conclude an inspection. The 483 is usually the initial action by FDA in an escalating process for enforcing compliance.

The 483 observations presented represent the opinion of the investigation team regarding what they have observed during the inspection. These observations are not always correct because they may not have seen other examples, or they have misunderstood what information was presented. You have an opportunity to provide final feedback on the investigators' understanding at the inspection close-out meeting. However, this is not the time to argue strongly about the observation made.

The 483 observations will then be reviewed by the FDA District Office management team (Inspection Supervisor, Compliance Manager, and/or District Director) to determine severity and follow-up actions. The observations will be reviewed within the context of the entire inspection report (called the Establishment Inspection Report or EIR) to ascertain agency concerns about product safety or overall compliance.

The FDA expects that the inspected firm will provide a response to the 483 within a couple of weeks. The adequacy of these response will often determine next actions by the FDA District Office.

In short, the FDA considers a 483 observation as documented evidence of non-compliance with GXP requirements. Multiple observations during one inspection, repeat observations, or similar observations between sites of the same company are considered patterns of non-compliance that can result in more severe regulatory action.

Is a 483 observation the same as a verbal observation made at the conclusion of an FDA inspection? Should they be treated differently by the inspected firm?

At the conclusion of many FDA inspections, the investigators may provide what they term "verbal observations" that are not included on the 483 form. In the past, there was no response to these expected. However, in recent years, it has become standard practice and, to a significant extent, an expectation that the firm will provide a written response to these observations. Though verbal observations do not have the regulatory status of written 483 observations, FDA does consider these items of potential GXP non-compliance and they will typically follow-up on them in future inspections. A failure to take these seriously or make needed enhancements will often result in them becoming 483 observations in subsequent inspections.

A verbal observation should be considered a "close call" or a call to action. It is possible that these items did not rise to the level of a 483 simply because the investigator had confidence that the firm would quickly correct potential issues. It is also not uncommon that if an FDA investigator would observe the same verbal item at another site of the same firm, it would be listed as a 483 observation, not a verbal one. Thus, it is imperative that you take verbal observations seriously, provide a written update in your response to FDA, and that you take action to remedy the concern at the site inspected and other sites within the company.

Should you provide a written response to the FDA District Office for verbal observations even if no 483 observations were issued?

Yes. Communicating to the District Office regarding actions taken for verbal observations demonstrates your ongoing commitment to continuously improve compliance and that you willingly provide updates to FDA regarding compliance issues. It also demonstrates the importance of being proactive in response to potential issues.

What is the significance of the 483 observation? How should I react when I receive one and what should be our response?

Not all 483 observations should be considered equal. Some represent a significant issue that could lead to product safety concerns or strong regulatory action. Other observations are less significant. However, our actions regarding observations should be the same for all.

Typically, the FDA investigators will prioritize the 483 observations by significance to them... more significant concerns will be listed first with less significant ones following. Additionally, an observation with multiple parts or multiple examples generally represents a more significant issue.

All 483 observations require a response provided to the contact individual at the FDA District Office. Key points to remember in a response include:

- Respond in a timely fashion, typically, within two weeks

- Keep the response simple and limit additional commentary unless it is necessary to provide context or explanation of the corrective action

- Do not use the 483 response to criticize the investigators

- Be specific on what action will occur, how it will be measured, and when it will be completed

- Respond globally – that is, extend the response to other associated functions or operations – do not limit your response to one specific example for one specific batch

- If applicable, describe what action will be taken to ensure that marketed products pose no safety or compliance risk (Remember: The number one concern of regulatory investigators is consumer safety!)

- Indicate when the District Office can expect an update on progress of the action if the actions are complex or long-term

- Express and re-affirm the commitment of your company to faithfully comply with all requirements of GXPs

- Offer to provide additional information to the District Office either in writing or in an in-person

> meeting, if that would enhance FDA understanding of your actions or compliance commitment

Your goals in providing a response are to demonstrate your commitment to GXP compliance, outline a specific plan of remediation, alleviate any potential concerns with product safety, and work toward establishing trust regarding your GXP compliance posture. Leave out anything else from your 483 response.

Is it reasonable to establish a goal of zero 483 observations?

It should always be your goal to fully and completely comply with all current GXP requirements. So, in those terms, a goal of zero 483 observations should be the target.

However, despite comprehensive training of FDA investigators, they rely upon individual opinions regarding what concerns are included on the 483, which might merit a verbal comment, and others with no comment. The experience and background of investigators matter regarding which items appear on the 483. So, to that extent, the appearance of minor 483 items should not be cause for an over-reaction.

Certainly, there are cases when the issuance of a 483 form should result in concerns. When observations appear that were easily preventable, which resulted from poor inspection management, or that indicate poor discipline should result in serious post-inspection actions. However, there should be room for grace when a 483 observation represents a questionable concern that can be easily addressed or when it represents a "new initiative" cited by FDA that could not have been anticipated.

How far should I go to avoid any 483 observations?
Should I work to avoid a 483 item at any expense?

What is it worth to avoid a single 483 observation? I was once asked that question by a manager concerned about financial costs for making facility improvements. Is it worth spending $1M on improving legacy production areas to avoid a 483 that cites the areas as inadequate?

GXP practitioners are frequently put in the position to financially justify compliance enhancements. The arguments might go something like this:

- Making that improvement will cost $1M

- If the FDA cites it as a 483 observation, we'll fix it then – it will likely not escalate into more severe FDA action

- If the FDA does not cite it, we have saved $1M

- If we save the $1M, we can use that money to purchase new laboratory equipment or hire that new employee you need to drive data integrity enhancements

- If we have to spend that $1M now, you will have to delay other projects or personnel additions you say will enhance compliance

- Where do you want to spend that $1M?

You can see how we often must make choices on how we spend limited finances. When faced with such decisions, I believe you have three choices:

- Fight for funding to do both

- Perform reduced enhancement in each area

- Conduct a risk assessment that formally identifies highest priority action needed – thus, you identify top priority for spending limited funds

Typically, if you know you cannot afford now to remediate both situations, a risk assessment will help identify where you should spend those limited resources.

What about repeat 483 observations? Are they treated more seriously by FDA?

Repeat 483 observations must be avoided. To FDA, the repeat observation indicates either the failure of the initial remedial action or a failure to commit the organization to GXP compliance. FDA often cites repeat observations in the escalation of enforcement, such as Warning Letters.

Because repeat observations can elicit such serious escalation, you need to take special precautions to complete all necessary actions on items, extend the action to related/similar situations, and be vigilant that issues do not recur.

Are 483 observations from other companies available for review? How should I react to 483 observations received by others?

Yes, you can often obtain 483 observations received by other companies. These can be requested via Freedom of Information Requests (FOI) to FDA or you can purchase services that provide summaries. Others can be obtained from colleagues, social media, or via request directly.

A 483 form from another company should be treated as a valuable opportunity to enhance compliance in your own operation. Utilize these "gifts" as inputs into your own compliance enhancement program and manage toward preventing the same item in your facility.

How can you tell if a 483 observation is serious? What should you do when you believe FDA is concerned about a serious non-compliance situation? What steps can you take to possibly avoid a 483 observation from escalating into a Warning Letter or worse?

Usually, you can discern after an inspection if the investigator believes you have a serious GXP non-compliance situation. You can often tell by the comments, demeanor, or length of the inspection. The number and extent of comments on the 483 can also be indicative of serious concerns.

When potential serious non-compliance concerns exist, you must take action to help alleviate concerns by the District Office management. A visit to the District Office to present, by hand, your response is often helpful. This meeting can be used to further your commitment to resolve issues and explain the extent of completed or planned actions. The attendance of a member of your senior management (e.g., President, Senior VP, etc.) can serve to further demonstrate the commitment by top management of the firm.

An in-person meeting with District Office management can also be effective in preventing further escalation of enforcement. I have seen cases in which a Warning Letter was avoided because this meeting was effective in demonstrating the effectiveness of actions taken in response to the 483.

In summary, the 483 (or global equivalent) is a serious document. It serves to document GXP non-compliance and initiate potentially escalating enforcement. Thus, our actions to avoid 483 items entirely, or at least to provide responsive and comprehensive action, can often head off more serious concerns.

Part Three

Everything you need to know for regulatory inspection success

10

A Contrarian's Approach to GXP Compliance and Inspection Readiness

Almost every day, a new approach for enhancing GXP compliance is proposed, espoused, or encouraged. Yet, our industry continues to experience problems with non-compliance. Some of these issues result only in adverse publicity for the recipient, though some result in potentially serious safety issues for consumers.

Is there anything new that can help us assess potential GXP concerns and, thus, drive compliance enhancement? I would like to pose a new way of thinking about compliance that can possibly stimulate a new way of looking at these issues. I call this the contrarian's approach to enhancing GXP compliance. You may have heard of contrarian investors… individuals that invest in companies experiencing bad news. A contrarian is someone that opposes or rejects popular opinion. In the world of compliance, a contrarian is not apt to automatically believe all the good audit reports they receive or the good inspection history of the site. The contrarian's approach to compliance involves looking for bad news, not merely looking for what is going well. The contrarian asks the truly hard questions of compliance.

Let's look at a few questions that can stimulate the contrarian's approach. Ask these example questions of your team to generate alternative viewpoints of your own current compliance position.

1. *If we have a recall next week, what will be the issue that caused it? Could we prevent it today if we knew it?* - When banks often look to assess their security, they enlist individuals that have previously robbed banks to seek their guidance. They will ask them to identify weak points which they might use to their advantage if they were attempting to plan a robbery of their bank. We can use the same approach when we look at compliance. If we could look into the future to see that compliance or quality issues occurred in our operation, what would it be? A formal risk assessment or FMEA analysis could potentially identify areas that require additional attention or remediation.

2. *If two individuals in your lab wanted to dry lab results, how could they do it given your current systems and protection of data? What would we have to do to prevent it?* - In a similar fashion, working to identify ways that individuals could collaborate to create laboratory results or overcome failing results might identify weak areas. Though it is unlikely that two individuals would collaborate to short-cut existing systems, that possibility requires that we examine the potential and implement remediation, whether through systems, processes, or people.

3. *What will be the primary concern noted on the next Warning Letter your firm receives? Do we*

have to accept that this will happen or can we change the future if we act today? – Hopefully, you have individuals in your organization that routinely review and assess FDA Warning Letters, FD-483's issued, etc. By knowing what issues are occurring and trending with regulators, you can be current when you assess your own operation. By honestly looking at your own operation and assessing the most likely source of a future issue, you are ahead of the game, so to speak. I have used this question many times in the past and each time, some individual identified some potential concern that was not already on our compliance enhancement list.

4. *If your only job was preventing the next batch failure, what actions would you take today? What would you do if your job was hanging in the balance?* – Let's take a common source of compliance issues as an example... mislabeling. If your entire career rested on preventing mislabeling events, what actions would you take? What would you do differently? What systems changes would be needed? In a group setting, this line of questioning will always result in a list of actions, some practical and some not so much. However, as you sort through the suggestions, you may identify some actions that can be done to enhance label control. By taking this approach for any potential quality or compliance concern, you can often root out new ideas that can be of value.

5. *If an angry employee wanted to sabotage a batch of product, how would they do it? Is it possible that one angry individual could destroy your*

reputation as a company? - Intentional sabotage is another area that, though you hate to consider it, should be discussed. Many companies have experienced such issues. By seeking potential systems or process weaknesses, you may identify opportunities for reducing this possibility.

6. *If someone wanted to hide your next stability (or sterility or environmental) failure, how would they do it? What systems must be defeated for an individual to hide an undesired result?* - Any system involving critical results that can be defeated by one individual represents an opportunity for assessment (and improvement). But, it is impossible to minimize risks in these systems unless you systematically seek to identify weaknesses.

7. *If an operator needed to make unauthorized and undetected changes to a manufacturing process, how would they do it? Can you devise systems to prevent it?* - Unless your manufacturing systems are completely automated, there is likely an opportunity for an operator to exert inappropriate discretion. For example, can an operator override operational parameters without detection? What discretion exists for semi-automated systems (e.g., ability to alter parameters or manually deviate) without documentation or detection?

These are only example questions. You could develop your own depending upon your operations. However, the concept is simple... if you wanted to foil your systems, could you do it and, if so, how? Or, if something bad was going to happen, what would it be and could you prevent it now, if you knew it? Using this approach was very productive in my past to identify new compliance enhancement opportunities.

GXP compliance is much more than following a checklist. It involves thinking beyond the regulations and seeking deeper, more complex answers. When you believe all the good audit reports you get each month, you are failing to recognize the underlying potential for disaster that could await. Think about using the contrarian's approach to identifying possibilities that, until today, have not been adequately considered.

11

Predictors of Regulatory GXP Inspection Success: How do you know if you should worry about your next inspection?

What are those factors or predictors of success for regulatory GXP inspections? Is it possible to know how your GXP inspection will go based on certain predictive criteria? The answer to these questions is challenging and, at best, difficult to say. I have seen some plants with excellent overall operations have significant issues raised during inspections and, of course, the opposite… sites that I know had numerous vulnerabilities, yet successful regulatory inspections.

However, my personal experience with over a hundred regulatory inspections has revealed several key items that I would term "predictors of success" that can help you ascertain the likely result of any specific plant inspection. Having this understanding is helpful for your existing sites, but might be especially helpful in assessing new suppliers, newly acquired operations, or for leaders when first assessing operations.

These items, in total, are predictors of regulatory GXP inspection success:

History of both site and company inspection results

If your company has a history of compliance concerns, even if no concerns for the specific site of concern have been noted, the scrutiny and likelihood of citations increases significantly. Global GXP investigators do review the compliance history of a site and related sites for the parent company before beginning an on-site regulatory inspection. Investigators have been trained to "connect the dots" and look for patterns across the company for non-compliance. Thus, any history of concerns at any location within the corporation elevates the risk for your site.

For example, one site in a multi-site organization has an FDA inspection that resulted in an FDA-483 observation. The response to the observation committed to implementation of a new procedure that will prevent a recurrence. However, when the FDA inspected a second facility, they found that the same procedural enhancement was not in place. Despite no quality issue occurring, the FDA cited the second site for failing to implement a global action to prevent the potential for the issue noted at the initial site. Likewise, when one site has significant issues, regulatory investigators will typically assume that similar issues exist at other sites and will, perhaps, look closer or deeper for these issues. Thus, when issues repeatedly exist at any location within a company, regulatory investigators will usually spend more time and effort to assure compliance at other sites.

Plant profile or risk level (e.g., product portfolio)

Regulators have clearly mandated that inspections and depth of review vary as the risk profile for the site increases. So, you can expect more frequent, more in-depth, and longer inspections for sites manufacturing parenteral pharmaceuticals than manufacturers of active pharmaceutical ingredient (API) manufacturers. So, generally, the higher the risk level of your products, the more complex, and the more safety risk posed (e.g., sterile versus non-sterile), the greater the potential for compliance concerns.

Number and severity of recent product quality or safety issues

Perhaps, the single most prevalent predictor of inspection success is the number and severity of recent product quality or safety issues, such as recalls, Field Alert Reports, or issues noted in the press. These events will assuredly receive significant attention during inspections and regulators will typically spend inordinate time reviewing these events. Their reviews will be deeper and more rigorous than for other systems and processes. Because of the concern with public safety, these issues are highly prone to non-compliance citations. Thus, the more of these you have experienced and the more severe risk to safety they get, the likelihood of non-compliance citations increases significantly.

Repetitive quality or compliance issues

One certain indicator of compliance concerns is the number of repeat issues noted in your quality systems. For example, how prevalent are repeat complaints, repeat product failures, repeat inspection citations, repeat investigations, etc. The fact that you have significant issues with repeat events indicates failing or inadequate root cause analysis and/or corrective and preventive action (CAPA) systems. If these are deemed inadequate, you can nearly be certain of non-conformance citations and subsequent concerns.

Regulatory agencies will commonly reflect the history of a site or company. For example, they may say, "... firm has a history of product sterility failures that has not been adequately investigated or corrected..." Thus, avoiding issues that allow a reference to a non-compliant history is critical for success.

Sophistication of quality and laboratory systems

Because of regulatory agency emphasis these days on data integrity, having sophisticated systems that remove human interaction will eliminate some of the concerns experienced by some firms. So, the more advanced these systems are, the less concern regarding data integrity SHOULD exist. Certainly, you must have robust validation of these systems, but having systems considered in the industry to be state-of-the-art (such as laboratory information management systems, electronic laboratory notebooks, enterprise quality management systems, etc.) diminishes some of the potential non-conformance concerns that we have all read about in public press.

Trends for quality metrics

Quality metrics are another "hot topic" for GXP regulators. If your systems include the tracking, trending, regular management review, and proactive action around findings, the risks for non-compliance citations during inspections are diminished, especially if trends indicate improving results.

On the contrary, adverse trends are "red flags" for investigators. It is imperative that firms develop strong systems for trending and tracking repetitive results. Then, there must be systems for identifying potential adverse trends followed by defined and documented actions.

It is typical in inspections today that investigators will request and review quality metric trending data early in the investigation. These data often dictate much of the remainder of the inspection. Thus, reviewing and reacting to such trends BEFORE an inspection is a critical predictor of success.

"Trust" quotient for Quality leaders

You may not see this item on any other list of top concerns in anticipation of regulatory inspections. But, in my extensive experience, the ability of regulators to develop a professional and trusting rapport with the site's Quality leaders is a profound advantage. So, if you can ascertain the "trust quotient" for your Quality leaders, you have a significant predictor of inspection success. In my opinion, factors that should be considered in this "trust

quotient" include: overall competence, demeanor under
pressure (cool and confident), "command" presence before
and during inspections (ability to instill professionalism,
confidence, and efficiency in others), and ability to
"connect" with others, including regulators. *So, in
summary, a leader with a high "trust quotient" will exhibit
these five "C's": competence, cool, confidence, command,
and connection.*

Proactive versus Reactive culture

You can get an accurate and quick prediction of inspection
success simply by gauging whether a site has a proactive
versus a reactive culture. Does the site already know its
vulnerabilities and is working to remedy them? Are there
systems to predict when issues are eminent and the
subsequent action to prevent them? Or, is the site simply
reacting to every individual event that occurs? I tend to
view this in terms of offensive versus defensive. Is the site
on the offensive to improve or is it simply in a defensive
shell to fix issues that go wrong? Identifying this can help
you predict inspection success.

Technical competence across key functions

A strong compliance culture is often marked by a high
level of technical competence across all functions, such as
Manufacturing, R&D, Regulatory Affairs, in addition to
Quality. When it is apparent that these other functions
have strength and understanding of GXP compliance and
exhibit a real sense of proactive compliance, you can be
certain that the overall compliance position for the site is

strong. This competence is especially apparent for individuals likely to interact with regulatory investigators. Identifying how these critical individuals convey confidence under pressure is a potential predictor of success because it often is an indicative of the robustness of data, systems, and operators they lead.

Cost cutting environment not balanced by continuous improvement

Finally, cost improvement is a real factor in today's competitive world. There is nothing wrong with a concerted effort to eliminate waste and improve costs within a GXP manufacturing arena. However, when the approach of these efforts is simply to cut costs without balancing it with continuous improvement (e.g., waste elimination, process improvement, working smarter, etc.), the risk for compliance concerns is elevated. The extent to which these efforts seek to improve costs through continuous improvement can be indicative of the culture of compliance at the site.

Certainly, these items alone cannot tell a complete story. We must certainly consider results of internal audits, industry/regulatory trends, unique vulnerabilities, quality costs, and robustness of quality systems. However, if you endeavor to create a relatively manageable list of items that, in concert, can predict the anticipated compliance posture of a site, this list of ten items can provide a highly correlated assessment of inspection risk. You can even quantify the relative risk of a site by grading the site in each of these ten items with a score that allows a rough comparison site-to-site (give each item a grade between 1 and 10, then total the score).

Understanding the relative risk of GXP inspection non-compliance can be important for allocating resources, allocating funding, or decision-making regarding compliance enhancement activities.

12

Regulatory GXP inspections: trials, tribulations, and successes

Inspections from regulatory agencies can be some of the most stressful periods ever experienced for some individuals and some plants. After all, these inspections can determine, literally, the future of the site. A successful pre-approval inspection can mean the difference between prosperity or struggles in many cases. For more established sites, a successful inspection can strengthen your compliance reputation or help foster a new culture of compliance. And, a solid inspection can serve as validation of the hard work expended to effectively manage compliance enhancement and inherent compliance risks.

Though much has been written about preparing for and managing inspections, I would like to pass along a few perspectives I have gained over the last few years. These hints might be helpful as you prepare for your next visit:

Confidence is a major contributor to successful inspection results

Let's face it... the end result of most inspections occurs, not because of tremendous management of the inspection, but because the site has prepared, individuals have diligently documented their work, and you have a stellar culture of compliance at the site. When you have prepared well, your inspection management team operates with more confidence. Investigators are trained to observe for this confidence and look for signs of concern or weakness. Being able to confidently present site results and a strong GXP compliance position significantly supports a successful inspection result.

How can you exude this confidence? What are some practical things that illustrate this confidence? Here are a few examples:

- Allow subject matter experts to freely answer questions by investigators during inspections. Certainly, you need to prepare these individuals beforehand and coach them on answering only the question asked. But, I have had many investigators comment that when we allowed these experts to speak directly and freely, it illustrated confidence in our systems, processes, and people that made a difference.

- Present information quickly and with as little screening as possible. When it appears that you spend too much time screening information presented during the inspection, the impression is that you have concerns that must be hidden.

- Don't allow the inspection to inappropriately disrupt site operations. If it appears that "everything must stop" during inspections, the impression is that you cannot manage the inspection without an extensive effort to control the message and information presented.

Managing the logistics of regulatory inspections is becoming more and more important

Regulatory investigators are becoming more and more demanding about the speed of producing documents and whether or not the site was completely forthcoming regarding answers to questions. With the implementation of new FDA Guidance documents, FDA is now more aggressive about what they have access to, how quickly documents are provided, and who and how questions are answered. Speed is becoming almost as important as accuracy during the actual inspection, though I would always choose the latter over the former.

Managing the investigator (or team) is essential

Because of the challenges posed by the need for speed and accuracy in producing information , it is becoming even more crucial that you effectively manage both the front- and back-rooms during inspections well. If you have not rehearsed this recently, it might be worth doing so again, especially if you have new individuals involved in the process. Understanding the mood and demeanor of the investigator is important, as well. Pay close attention to body language, expressions, and comments made by the investigator as the inspection progresses.

You must also be prepared for an investigation team that splits into separate groups to minimize time while maximizing inspection coverage. I know of one example in which a site was visited by 12 investigators split into three different inspection teams at one time. The site was so inundated that lower level individuals were playing key roles in the inspection that they were never trained or prepared to handle.

Remain calm and professional despite potential threats or intimidation

I have heard from industry colleagues examples in which an investigator made a number of comments during the inspection about demanding a recall, escalating items to the FDA manager, or even going public with negative information. Knowing that the investigator does not have the authority for much of this makes it essential that you remain calm and professional and not lose your focus. It is possible that an FDA investigator would occasionally use such techniques to get the plant to share information that they would normally not share. However, remaining calm can help shift the inspection back to a less stressful relationship.

I know of one inspection recently in which the investigator demanded the presentation of requested information within five minutes. If it was not presented during this time, she threatened the site with a "non-cooperation" or "withholding information" citation. Do not be intimidated by these comments! A site is allowed adequate time to secure, review, and present information. Do not feel that such intimidation can stand.

Do not be pressed into making unnecessary commitments

You must never make hasty commitments during an inspection without full knowledge and approval from your senior management. The FDA investigator may attempt to get a verbal commitment from you that they can include in their report. It is important to always state that you will respond appropriately when needed and after full collaboration with all functions necessary.

You can easily identify examples of "on the spot" commitments by reviewing FDA Warning Letters or FD-483 documents. Typically, these state something like "the Quality Assurance Manager stated that this situation should not have occurred, and the procedure will be changed to reflect actual practice" or something similar. Avoid such commitments! An investigation and discussion is needed before making any commitment other than "we will review this situation and provide an update, when applicable" or something similar. It could be that the procedure was correct, but other mitigating factors were present. You must also consider global aspects of any such commitment (e.g., the impact on other functions, sites, or processes).

Focus on the science, adherence to GXPs, and patient safety

You need to remember that the first priority of FDA or other regulatory investigators is to ensure public safety. With this in mind, you can often produce information that can negate the concerns of the investigator. When they realize that there is no public safety concern, the level of alarm often immediately diminishes.

In such cases, you may have to provide more or different information than you would normally provide. For example, to make a scientific case, involving the technical expert to make the point may be necessary. Let me illustrate... A deviation in the manufacturing process at an early step for producing an API may require an explanation by the R&D process development scientist to help the investigator understand that the impact of the deviation had no impact on the chemistry, process control, or ultimate purity of the final product. The bottom line is that you may need to consider sharing information not normally shared in cases where the science makes an overwhelming case.

Thoroughness of your investigation reports remains important

Every investigation involves the review of investigations (OOS, Exceptions, Complaints, etc.). This is a focus for every investigator. Thus, you must remain ever diligent in conducting these thoroughly, documenting all your actions completely, and ensuring that the reports tell a full story.

Inadequate investigation report citations appear on a high percentage of GXP deficiency reports. You simply cannot ignore completeness and accuracy in this area. I highly recommend that an independent review of these investigations occur in preparation for regulatory inspections. Certainly, these will be complete and thorough when initially approved. However, these independent reviews can help ensure that they can withstand regulatory review AND these reviews can provide an opportunity to supplement these reports with information that enhances their robustness prior to the inspection.

You should have a significant team to back you up

Inspections often move into areas outside the responsibility of the inspected site that requires expert assistance. For example, questions may arise regarding regulatory filings that require assistance from the off-site Regulatory Affairs function. Or, you may need R&D assistance to answer detailed questions for products under review. Remember that you must defer to these experts, when necessary. Attempting to provide answers without proper input can result in issues. One note of caution, though, is to ensure that you prepare any individuals from outside the site that speaks with the investigators. Prepare them in advance similarly to how you might prepare a site subject matter expert before bringing them into the inspection.

A successful regulatory inspection is a team effort, not merely a management effort by members of the quality function. Preparing all functions that could be called upon and engaging them as active team members can help ensure their availability and positive participation during the inspection.

Stay focused to the end

Some regulatory inspections can continue for weeks. During an extended inspection, your team may become "comfortable" with the investigator and, as a result, let down their guard. You must be diligent and focused all the way to the end! I have seen inspections that went very well all the way until the last day when significant issues were raised. Allowing team members breaks during an extended inspection can help keep them fresh and alert. Staying focused throughout an extended inspection is a challenge, but you need to remain on-guard and at-the-top-of-your-game all the way to the end.

Most inspections have moments of trial and tribulation. But, if you remain diligent and focused, you have a greater probability of best representing your site and its GXP performance. Your ability to adequately prepare and foster an ongoing compliance culture now will pay off the next time your site receptionist calls with the exciting news, "Two individuals from the FDA have just arrived." Good luck on your next inspection!

13

Behind the scenes of a regulatory GXP inspection: Questions and Answers

Many that are new to regulatory inspections (and, most global regulatory inspections would be similar) and even some that have been around the block are not aware of some of the interactions that occur during these inspections. I have been personally involved in over 100 of these inspections myself, most of which I was the lead company representative. Plus, I have a number of friends and acquaintances that are or were regulatory investigators, so I think I can paint a pretty accurate picture of what really goes on during these inspections.

Following are ten sets of questions/answers around typical regulatory investigators and the inspections they conduct. Keep in mind that these answers are for TYPICAL situations, not all.

1. *What preparation occurs by the investigator prior to the presentation of the final report (or FDA-483 form) for an inspection at your facility?* - Most investigators do spend time preparing ahead of the inspection. In some cases, this preparation is extensive and may require a week or more. Investigators will examine the firm's file and review the most recent inspection and any company

responses or correspondence. They will note the verbal recommendations made during the last inspection. They will also review any Field Alert Reports, recalls, or other issues communicated to the District Office or agency office. Additionally, many investigators will review results of inspections for other manufacturing sites in other locations for your company. For example, if an FDA Warning Letter was issued at one of your sister sites, the investigator will likely review the issues noted and the company response to determine if follow-up at your site is needed. Don't assume that the investigator merely walks into your facility "cold." They will likely be very aware of your compliance position and have a list of potential concerns or issues that they will examine during their time on-site.

2. ***What is the motivation or driving factor for the typical regulatory investigator? Are they looking to make a name for themselves to advance their own career or is it something else?*** - I think many individuals in industry assume that regulatory investigators advance their careers based on the number of GXP citations they provide. This is not the case. Most good investigators are motivated by their desire to ensure the safety of the consuming public. They are concerned with any GXP violations, but especially those that could harm a consumer. Their primary focus is whether our products are acceptable as measured by their safety, purity, effectiveness, labeled strength, and labeled identity. In short, they are most concerned with product quality. They may cite more minor GXP violations, but their primary interest is to ensure that we

perform in an overall manner that will prevent a negative impact to our consuming public. Sure, there are some investigators that are looking for ways to enhance their own standing within the agency, but more investigators are intent on serving the public by ensuring we do what we should and what we said in our regulatory filings.

3. ***Is it really possible to influence the outcome of the regulatory investigation by how the investigation team manages the investigation?*** - The answer to this question is a clear and definitive "Yes!" I have seen many inspections turn positive or negative simply by how they were managed. When the investigator develops a trust in the management team, feels that the team is open and honest, and believes that the information provided is accurate, the inspection will almost always be more collaborative, positive, and productive. When the investigator feels the company's inspection team is deceptive (trying to hide something), manipulative (screening out negative information), or hindering the inspection (by preventing access to information or facilities), the inspection almost always turns negative. In fact, when the investigator believes any of these is the case, they can now take even more aggressive action that is supported by more recent regulations. So, be open, be honest, work diligently to share everything requested, and seek to demonstrate integrity in managing the inspection.

4. ***What does the regulatory investigator do with all the documentation they collect?*** - Most of the mountains of documentation collected during an inspection is destroyed after the inspection is

closed. So, what purpose does it serve? There are really three purposes for the documentation collected during an inspection:

- To allow further study of potential compliance concerns during the time between on-site visits during a multi-day inspection

- To document compliance (or non-compliance) activities noted during the inspection (e.g., proof of concerns noted in any potential FDA-483 observations or citations)

- To facilitate the final report after the inspection (Establishment Inspection Report or EIR)

5. ***What does the regulatory investigator do between leaving your facility for the day and arrival the next at your door?*** - Most investigators spend some time reviewing their observations for the day before arriving the next day. If they are traveling to your site, it is not uncommon for investigators to spend much of their evenings reviewing documentation, making notes about potential concerns, and preparing for their review the next day. In many cases, the investigator is communicating with their supervisor or Compliance Office about findings and the direction of the inspection for coming days. It is the rare investigator that does no preparation before arriving the next day.

6. ***Would you rather have a highly experienced and knowledgeable investigator inspect your facility or one that is less experienced and less knowledgeable? Why?*** - Personally, I would rather have an experienced and knowledgeable investigator inspect my site. These investigators can more

accurately and quickly focus on potential issues,
their experience allows them to better understand
what we do and why, and they tend to need less
background information to grasp the concepts of
more complex operations and activities. And, these
investigators are less prone to citing less significant
issues. However, because of their experience, they
are more likely to quickly identify more significant
issues that could evade a less experienced
investigator. So, depending upon your situation,
there are advantages to either. Nonetheless, we have
no choice in who inspects our facilities, so this is
something we have little ability to influence.

7. ***How have regulatory inspections and investigators
   changed over the last 40 years?*** - Many years ago,
   regulatory investigators all covered many different
   regulated industries, such as pharmaceuticals,
   medical devices, food, blood, medicated feeds, etc.
   They had to learn the regulations and have adequate
   knowledge of all of these to properly function.
   Today, they tend to be experts in one industry. For
   example, now, investigators tend to focus on
   pharmaceuticals or medical devices or foods. Thus,
   they have the opportunity to learn about varying
   packaging techniques, dosage forms, and
   manufacturing techniques in a way that allows
   greater depth of expertise. Additionally, regulatory
   agencies tends to recruit more individuals with
   advanced degrees or industry experience. Agency
   training programs also provide more in-depth
   knowledge than 40 years ago. So, on the whole,
   investigators today tend to have more knowledge
   about their specific areas of expertise than the
   investigators of the past that had to have more

breadth. As a result, investigations today are more focused and directed. For example, investigations often focus on specific systems. So, an investigator that has just inspected other firms have a solid basis of comparison to assess whether we are fulfilling "current" expectations.

8. *What causes a regulatory investigator to lose sleep at night and why?* - Regulatory investigators take their responsibilities very seriously! The thing that concerns them most is failing to detect GXP violations that ultimately result in safety or health concerns. They never want to be personally responsible for missing a potentially serious issue during an inspection. Thus, you can see why most are so diligent in focusing on issues that most clearly could harm consumers (e.g., data integrity, sterility, foreign contamination, labeling, dosing, etc.).

9. *Why do we see so many different approaches taken by regulatory investigators (e.g., some want to be collaborative; some are aggressive; some use inspection guides; some merely follow the flow; etc.)?* - Though regulatory inspection guidelines are pretty specific in what investigators should consider examining during an inspection, they do not remove the ability of investigators to use their individual talents to conduct investigations. As a result, some focus on procedures, some on data, some on checklists, some on manufacturing, etc. And, the individual personality of the investigator will often determine the flow and collaboration of the inspection. Typically, the investigator is patient and collaborative as long as you provide information

openly and efficiently. I have witnessed a few investigators that are not so patient and collaborative, no matter how the inspection is managed. In these cases, you must remain professional, calm, and continue working efficiently. You must not allow that rare rude or impulsive investigator to intimidate you into mistakes or misstatements.

10. *What is the goal of the typical regulatory investigator?* - For them, what constitutes a successful inspection? Most investigators are just like us... they have a job to do and simply want to get it done thoroughly and completely. They are not normally trying to do more than that. We must realize, though, the gravity of their job which is to protect the ultimate consumer of our products. We should attempt, as much as possible, to help them accomplish that task, yet without exposing more information than is requested. Realizing their goal can help us manage the inspection and how we interact with the investigator.

Hopefully, this has helped you understand better the typical regulatory GXP inspection and the inspection approach. When we better understand what is really occurring, we can better manage the flow and content of the inspection.

14

Things you should never say during a regulatory GXP inspection

Sometimes we learn best by seeing what NOT to do. I have accumulated a few of the comments heard in during my many years in healthcare industries. Some of these were actually said during a regulatory inspection (not by my choice, believe me!), but many others were voiced during mock regulatory inspections or audits. Each instance was an opportunity for coaching outside the context of the inspection or audit. Despite our best efforts to train our teams on how to respond to regulatory questions, it is common for an individual (not all inexperienced either) to make an off-beat comment in the heat of the inspection that they know was wrong.

So, for your entertainment and, hopefully, use in your own regulatory inspection training, here are the comments:

1. *We had to release that lot, it was the only one we had, and we needed to keep production running.*

2. *Our micro lab is across the street. Would you like us to take you over there right now?*

3. *We are still amazed at how sharp last year's inspector was.*

4. *If you think this is bad, you should see how our sister plant down the street does it.*

5. *We have no idea how that happened!*

6. *The only guy that knew how to do that retired last year. We'll give him a call during the lunch break.*

7. *We'll show that area to you later after we finish cleaning it up.*

8. *This OOS was unusual because almost all our problems are due to unclean glassware.*

9. *Give me just a minute. I think they keep that password here in the bottom drawer.*

10. *Really, what's the big deal. All we're talking about is a few complaints!*

11. *We keep all the SOPs in the supervisor's office. If we kept them here in the production area, they would be a mess.*

12. *If we had known you were coming, we would have cleaned the place up.*

13. *That's not so bad, we've done a whole lot of things worse.*

14. *I don't know for sure, but I assume.....*

15. *I'm sure you won't understand this but let me try to make it simple for you.*

16. *I'm not sure, but let me take a guess....*

17. *Before you leave, can we show you a new system that we've been implementing? We're very proud of it.*

18. *Actually, we're pretty lucky that it wasn't any worse than that.*

19. *I know you only asked for this, but I brought along several related documents that you might find helpful.*

20. *We had to make a number of changes during our process validation study, but we eventually got it to work.*

21. *That test method is so complex that only one or two of our analysts can get the right numbers.*

22. *We had results all over the place, but we're sure that the result that met our specifications was right.*

23. *We have quality personnel in production only during first shift because we don't have a second shift crew.*

24. *We think our interpretation of that statute is probably more current than yours.*

25. *You know what they say, 'The end justifies the means.'*

Just a few take-aways from these comments:

- Be sure you continually re-enforce that individuals should just answer the questions asked and offer only information specifically requested (unless approved by the inspection manager)

- Never hide requested information from the investigator – however, you are also under no obligation to expose issues not requested

- When in doubt, the less said, the better – don't be afraid of silence

- Never offer to show an area, system, document, data, or anything else not specifically requested, no matter how proud of it you might be – the only exception is if this might help you make a point raised by other questions asked

- When a GXP violation has been identified, don't make it worse by trying to justify your actions or by revealing other related issues – take your medicine and correct other issues internally

- Always respect the investigator, no matter what happens or how you feel – they are just trying to do their job to protect our ultimate consumers

- If possible, review the questions and what will be said to investigators outside the room before allowing individuals to speak directly – this is especially true for individuals less experienced with inspections

15

Actions you should take during those critical first 24 hours after closing a regulatory GXP inspection

Much has been written and said about preparing for an FDA inspection (or other regulatory inspection). However, I have not seen anything written which describes what actions are needed during the critical first 24 hours after the inspection closes. Certainly, you need to begin preparing any needed response to the inspection results, but there are a number of significant actions you must take during the first day post-inspection that could very well determine your success or failure for the next inspection.

Let's take a look at those critical "first 24 hours" actions:

1. ***Communicate results to management*** - Most firms have a policy or standard practice that communication to management regarding inspection results is required immediately after the closing conference. This is important. However, it is also important to communicate to management any other details or actions that could elicit future

concerns (such as a Warning Letter) or items that should be addressed in other similar facilities. FDA expects that actions taken be global in application, so other sites should be made aware quickly of any issues that could apply there.

2. ***Thank individuals involved in managing the inspection*** – It is essential that one of the first actions you take after the inspection is to personally thank those that worked so diligently to manage the inspection well. Those in the front room, back room, subject matter experts, and those working behind the scenes need to be identified and thanked for their work and actions leading up to and through the inspection. Many of these individuals worked far beyond their normal work schedule during the inspection and, in some cases, delayed vacations, missed family events, or postponed other important work to ensure the inspection was successful. Consider doing something special for key individuals, such as a gift certificate for two to dinner. Take the time very quickly after the inspection close-out to thank them both privately and publicly.

3. ***Thank the entire site for supporting the inspection*** – A successful inspection result is always tied to the diligence and efforts of the entire site. A site-wide communication summarizing the basic results of the inspection and thanking the site for their efforts goes a long way to encourage future compliance and improvement activities.

4. ***Begin laying the groundwork for the next inspection*** – In most cases, the data and information that will be reviewed during the next inspection

begins the day after the inspection closes. The day after an inspection is NOT the time to become lax or less diligent. Emphasize to your inspection management team, the site management team, and all individuals at the site that it is important to remain diligent and exercise a high level of compliance every day and in every activity. This communication can be included in the site-wide communication mentioned above, a site-wide meeting, video, or other means, but it is important that you emphasize continued and ongoing diligence.

5. *Initiate actions to capture and sustain positive momentum* – In many cases, the teamwork, effort, and cross-functional camaraderie experienced during an inspection is unmatched by any other activity that occurs at the site. For the period of the inspection, everyone is singly focused on a positive inspection result. Utilize this momentum and work to sustain it. Celebrate this success with a pizza party or other event. Utilize this momentum to tackle other important site projects. Quick action can ensure that you don't merely get "back to normal" the day after the inspection closes.

6. *Assign responsibilities and actions for any needed formal response* – The inspection may result in the need for a formal response back to FDA (or other regulatory agency). Verbal or written items should be addressed comprehensively, so beginning action early and assigning responsibilities for initial or immediate actions are needed early. These do not need to be completed in the first day, but

individuals should begin these activities as soon as possible after the closing.

7. ***Assign responsibilities and actions for any new "lessons learned" or "close calls"*** - Most inspections result in "close calls" or "lessons learned." Assigning responsibilities for actions associated with these should also be made soon after the closing. Speedy action may improve quality, improve compliance, or reduce other risks.

The key point is that it is good to celebrate the conclusion of a regulatory inspection, especially if the result is positive. However, there are some actions you should take within the first workday after the inspection to ensure a smooth transition back to "normal", to ensure that key contributors are recognized, and to ensure that actions are taken to set the stage for an even better result on the next inspection.

Part Four

The future of compliance and regulatory inspections

16

Perspectives on healthcare from a patient's viewpoint

I spent almost all of my working career involved in looking at the healthcare patient as a customer or end-user. Though we do our best to consider our products and care from the patient's perspective, it just isn't the same as when *you* are that person in the hospital bed whose life and well-being depend upon those same products and services.

A couple of years ago, I found myself looking up from the hospital bed again. That time, I had a total knee replacement. The procedure was relatively quick (about 45 minutes) and the hospital stay short (one night). But, it was amazing how such an event allows exposure to the entire healthcare system, end-to-end. For this surgery, I had x-rays, diagnostic blood tests, surgery, anesthesia, hospital care, physical therapy, home visits, pharmaceutical products, and medical device products that illustrate both the good and not-so-good of our healthcare system.

I would like to cover a few insights and perspectives that I have gained from this and prior experiences. I think it is worth sharing what I have learned and observed that might benefit others.

Everyone loves to hate opioid pain medications... until they need them!

Opioid pain medications are on everyone's evil drug list these days. While it is true that many ills in society are due to the addicting nature of these products (e.g., morphine, oxycodone, hydrocodone, etc.), try having major surgery without them! These products have an amazing ability to temper or eliminate the severe pain associated with surgery. I often found myself watching the clock in anticipation of my next pain-relieving dose. Thus, it is easy to see how one might become overly dependent on them. Finding that balance between benefits and risks is a challenge that we must somehow achieve. I credit a large degree of the success of my surgery to opioids. For without them, I would not have been able to withstand the physical therapy that differentiates success from failure of a total knee replacement.

Healthcare is becoming more patient-focused and outcome-based

I have definitely seen a shift in medical care toward results. Before choosing my surgeon, I studied his success and complication rates through internet searches. His standard protocol for post-op rehabilitation has changed to accommodate new research on eventual outcomes. Insurance companies have become much more focused on ultimate results and will withhold payment on treatments that are not statistically justified. Entire healthcare teams and individuals continuously seek input from customers (e.g., patients) through surveys, opinion polls, and feedback mechanisms. Of course, some of this outcome-based emphasis is good and some not-so-good. When it is directed toward continuous improvement of care and patient satisfaction, it is certainly good. However, when merely used to limit or shift costs and reimbursement, it falls short of desirable.

Strong teamwork and highly coordinated processes are replacing the silo treatment approach of the past

For my most recent knee replacement surgery, I was amazed at the end-to-end teamwork evident. My past experience was that each phase of the process (surgeon, administrative, physical therapy, communication, etc.) was handled as a stand-alone entity. The surgeon did his work, then passed you along to the physical therapy team, etc. However, in this case, every piece of the process was coordinated and tied to each other piece. Prior to my hospital discharge, home visit appointments were made with a nurse and physical therapist. Everything needed for recovery was arranged and scheduled. A training session occurred before surgery that included my "joint coach" to ensure we both knew what to expect and what we needed to do together to be successful. I was pleasantly surprised how each element of process was integrated with each of the others.

Though patients have become more educated on healthcare options and expectations, every individual journey is unique

I have to admit that I probably read too much information on total knee replacement surgery before my own procedure. Though most of the information available on the internet spoke to the positive outcome expected, there are always horror stories that make you second guess your decision. Nonetheless, a patient these days can watch videos of actual surgeries, get a report card on the surgeon and hospital, get hundreds of testimonies from others that have experienced the same surgery, and be highly knowledgeable on all aspects of the procedure. You can even "shop" various knee joint manufacturers for options and benefits in much the same way you might shop for a new car online! Despite this vast amount of available knowledge, the outcome and recovery for each patient is unique. My progress is different than anyone else that ever had this surgery. Thus, all of this newfound knowledge doesn't replace listening to the advice of the surgeon, therapists, and adhering to the program they outline.

A shift to modern analytics-based care is occurring

Every individual I encountered throughout my journey was extremely knowledgeable and professional. However, it is evident that the modern approach, based strongly on analytics, trending, and remote monitoring, has not yet been fully embraced. Most have adapted well to this approach. However, some still prefer the "old days" of patient care and personalized service. I think this scenario plays out in every discipline and every field... some individuals prefer "the way we did it in the old days" to today's approach. Both approaches are effective, but, perhaps, both are not equally efficient.

Everyone is a specialist

It has been clear to me that specialization has become increasingly important in healthcare. My surgeon specialized in knees and hips. Another of my procedures was performed by an orthopedist that specializes in shoulders. Hospital visits are handled by "hospitalists". It seems that even the nursing staff has migrated toward specialization. Though most of us still utilize a primary physician, care outside ordinary well-care or normal illnesses is typically outsourced to a specialist. Knowing this should be a factor to everyone in the healthcare industry.

I think it is good to occasionally consider how the healthcare industry is changing. By doing so, we might conclude that changes to other pieces of the industry must also change (e.g., R&D, manufacturing, quality, engineering, etc.). When you look at the key six points I have outlined above, you'll find these key topics that apply to everyone in every industry:

- *risk/benefit assessment* – seeking an appropriate balance
- *outcome-based results* – adding value
- *strongly integrated teamwork* – collaborating for the ultimate good of the customer (patient)
- *continuous learning* – educating yourself, staying current, seeking innovation
- *embracing change* – a willingness to accept a new approach, especially when the value is demonstrated
- *specialization versus generalization* – enhancing our personal value by enhancing our expertise

So, the question we should be asking ourselves is, "Am I doing what I can to enhance to ultimate experience for my patients, customers, coworkers, family, or associates?" I think there is something here that can help each of us become more valuable to our company and to others that we serve.

17

What will inspections be like in the future?

What will regulatory inspections be like in the future? Will they be the same as we've seen in the last decade or two or will they dramatically change? We have seen a shift toward systems-based inspections, but will that continue?

The US FDA and other regulatory agencies have indicated in recent years that they now attempt to conduct and schedule on-site inspections based on the risk profile of the facility. Facilities producing aseptic products will have a higher risk score and, thus, be subject to more frequent and rigorous inspections than API manufacturers. To a large degree, this makes sense. The impact of a sterility assurance issue, in theory, would have a greater potential for product safety issues than, for example, an impurity issue in an API... or would it? Despite efforts to classify facilities based on risk, a one-size-fits-all approach for determining frequency and depth of inspections based on product classification and risk profile is tenuous.

Another recent inspection trend is the effort to classify facilities (another risk-based approach) based on quality performance data. FDA has been working for several years now on collecting manufacturing and quality performance data from manufacturers. Then, based on the FDA review of these data, facilities with determined higher risks would receive greater inspectional attention. Several trial attempts have occurred in which manufacturer data has been shared and reviewed by FDA, but, thus far, efforts to standardize information has proven extremely difficult. For example, can accurately compare data from one solid dosage manufacturer that has mostly direct compression products with another that produces more complex, granulated products? Or, how do you compare one firm that manufacturers only one type of product with another that produces liquids, solids, and sterile APIs in the same facility? The complexity of developing a standardized approach for sharing complex data with FDA, creating an approach for objectively reviewing those data, then establishing criteria for ranking manufacturing risk in such a way that provides meaningful criteria for conducting inspections remains a challenge. Industry groups have also attempted to collaborate with FDA, but, at this point, no specific systems or guidance on the use of shared data to classify manufacturing site performance is in use.

The other recent shift regarding inspections has been the use of specialists that focus on one type of regulated product. Over the past 50 years, most FDA investigators were trained to provide inspectional coverage on all types of products. For example, an investigator may inspect a drug plant this week, a medical device manufacturer the week after, and a food plant the week after that. Being a generalist meant that investigators must be trained and experienced in all types of FDA-regulated products which diluted the ability of any one investigator to specialize in all products. Today, most drug plant inspections are conducted by an investigator that only inspects drug facilities. Likewise, specialists cover medical devices, APIs, foods, medicated feeds, blood products, etc. This specialization trend is likely to become the standard, thus, investigators will require less training and less time becoming familiar with products.

Some efforts and discussions occurred during the Covid-19 pandemic regarding remote inspections. Is it possible to request and review extensive data, procedures, protocols, and reports remotely before deciding to visit in person? Could some operations be reviewed via remote video system? Such a system would also enhance opportunities to increase foreign inspections without increasing costs for personnel and travel extensively.

Regardless of the use of data provided to agencies, the use of specialists, and remote reviews, most inspections over the next decade or two will likely remain dominated by on-site inspections by multiple, trained and experienced investigators. Thus, our ability to prepare, react professionally to inspection needs, manage relationships, and ensure ongoing high-level performance of all manufacturing and testing personnel will remain critical for successfully navigating GXP compliance.

Conclusions

Many pages ago, I outlined my objectives for this work:

1. *Education* - To help compliance practitioners teach others the importance of GXP compliance and create an enhanced culture of compliance

2. *Focus* - To provide focus on GXP compliance activities that are important and, thus, stop doing activities that provide no GXP compliance value

3. *Readiness* - To provide guidance on compliance and inspection readiness activities that focus on the "majors" and minimize activities are meaningless

4. *Outcomes* - To provide tools and advice that enhance success of regulatory inspections and management of inspection outcomes

5. *Future* - To provide perspectives and guidance on the future of regulatory inspections and activities that need to begin now

I hope we have made some progress helping you in each of these areas.

GXP compliance is in many ways a moving target. New Guidance documents are issued routinely. Initiatives to harmonize with global regulatory agencies and their individual requirements pose an ongoing challenge. New technology brings with it new opportunities to educate others, fine-tune our analytical capabilities, reduce human discretion, and automate processes. And, we can expect more change in the future as artificial intelligence emerges to aid regulatory reviews, manage manufacturing operations, and monitor field performance of our healthcare products. All of this, along with simultaneous cost control initiatives, makes GXP compliance more difficult, yet more rewarding when done well.

So, with all these challenges facing us daily, where should we focus our compliance enhancement efforts? Should we focus most on people? Or, technology? Or, perhaps, systems and equipment? What is most important?

Certainly, the answer to that question is unique for every individual organization. As FDA speakers like to say, "It depends." Your primary focus should always be in the area in which your organization is most vulnerable or the one that poses the greatest risk. However, do not forsake the people side of the business. Despite the temptation to believe that systems and technology will solve most of your problems, we must still rely on people to make things happen correctly. Let me provide a couple of anecdotes:

- I once had a boss that managed a complex operation consisting of aseptically filled products, solid dosage products, and other product types in one facility. He used to say, "If I could choose the best aseptic filling personnel in the world, I think I could produce sterile product with the line set up in the parking lot. Without the best people, you couldn't attain sterile product in the best facility ever built." Certainly, he was using hyperbole in this discussion, but his point was that for critical operations, such as aseptic processing, you must have the right people with the right experience doing the right job or you simply cannot expect to be successful.

- A former colleague left our company and moved to become VP, Operations at another operation producing pharmaceutical products. After a few months, he called me and said, "I have a real problem here. I cannot get anything we produce released. Any deviation, exception, or minor excursion results in product rejection without consideration of an investigation or other alternatives." My immediate intuition suggested that his Quality Unit was on the inexperienced side and, short of more experience, could not become comfortable defending a "perfect" batch.

Certainly, being conservative when dealing with GXP compliance is admirable. But, as GXP professionals, we must balance the need for tight GXP compliance with the basic business need of survival and being profitable. If everything in our business was black or white, our jobs would be easy. In fact, we wouldn't be needed!

Learning to become comfortable operating in the gray areas is what defines a great GXP professional. Finding a way to identify, assess, and evaluate the impact of imperfections in documentation, equipment, operations, or results in a manner that still adheres to the rigidity of GXPs makes our job hard... and it is what makes it, quite possibly, the most gratifying of careers.

It is easy to get caught up in the trap of continuing to perform GXP activities because we have always done them without questioning the value of those activities. I hope you can give yourself permission to ask, "Is there any value in what I'm doing? If not, what changes if we stop it? Is there a way to get the same result, yet do this in a different, easier way?" Take the opportunity to question what doesn't make sense.

I hope you have also gleaned possible new approaches or techniques for preparing for, managing, or responding to regulatory inspections through our journey here together. When you find a nugget of truth from any reading or any presentation that you can apply in your own operation, the effort becomes worthwhile.

Finally, I hope you will find value in the recommendation section provided immediately following this section. These recommendations are based on the material provided and may inspire you to make significant and needed improvements in your own operations.

Best of luck to you as your own GXP compliance journey continues. I have to say that I can still feel the excitement that occurs when you get the call from your facility receptionist, "Some individuals from the FDA are here to see you in the lobby." Perhaps even more exciting is the celebrations that occur after the close-out meeting of a successfully completed inspection. I recall that most facilities are never more unified, directed, and motivated as when an inspection occurs. Enjoy the journey and never forget why you do what you do... the ultimate patient is counting on you and has placed their trust in you to provide safe and effective products. Don't let that man, woman, or child down!

Recommendations

Chapter 1: Quality and Compliance Matter

1. Consider an assessment (or at least a discussion) as to whether, in your operation, you are:

   a. Doing more than should be expect for GXP compliance

   b. Acting faster than pragmatic GXP compliance would suggest is necessary

   c. Seeking to perform at a level higher than others unnecessarily

2. If the answer to any of the prior questions is "yes", determine what actions might be needed to ensure more value in GXP compliance activities across the company.

Chapter 2: The relationship of company culture to compliance culture

3. Assess the compliance culture of your company by asking the following questions:

   a. Is there evidence that there is a commitment to compliance as displayed by management?

   b. How does our management react when things go wrong?

   c. Is there evidence that, as a company, we are commitment to "doing the little things right"?

4. If you find, through the prior questions, that there is evidence that your company culture is not supportive of a strong compliance culture, discuss actions that can occur to enhance the culture.

Chapter 3: Educating management: How much adulteration is too much?

5. Review with top management the responsibilities of management, benefits of compliance, and regulatory agency enforcement options (even if top management is supportive, a routine review of these is valuable).

6. Highlight the competitive landscape regarding GXP compliance to senior management.

7. Demonstrate the "value" of compliance by reviewing the cost of non-compliance, direct financial impact of compliance, and the indirect financial impact of compliance.

8. Re-enforce the importance of "internal" and "external" reputation regarding GXP compliance.

Chapter 4: Enhancing compliance in a cost-conscious environment

9. Identify and prioritize "untouchables" regarding GXP compliance.

10. Re-examine prior compliance enhancement commitments to determine if newer initiatives have made them obsolete.

11. Conduct a formal risk management assessment to identify compliance improvement opportunities through ranking of risks.

12. Evaluation opportunities to maximize utilization of data trending to assess performance rather than react to individual excursions (e.g., environmental monitoring data).

13. Assess all compliance operations to determine the potential to reduce or eliminate waste in the categories of defects, processing, overproduction, waiting, motion, transport, inventory, or underutilized human resources.

14. Evaluate opportunities to redeploy resources (e.g., see redeployment strategies discussion in this chapter).

15. Take an honest inventory of short-term thinking, short-term actions, or short-term cultural biases that limit efficiency or effectiveness of GXP compliance activities.

16. Ensure that employee engagement/involvement opportunities exist around improvement of costs for compliance.

Chapter 5: When relentless becomes reckless

17. Discuss or assess your approach to compliance. Is it relentless (meaning a diligent, persistent

approach to improved compliance) or is it more closely related to reckless (meaning careless, impulsive, reactive, or irresponsible)? What action is needed?

Chapter 6: Dispelling GXP myths

18. Assess the 10 myths discussed in this chapter. Be honest about whether your company views on compliance or inspections inhibit efficiency or effectiveness of your compliance efforts. Then, determine what actions might be needed to regulate these views.

Chapter 7: Non-value added, feel-good GXP activities that do nothing to advance compliance

19. Assess the non-value added examples discussed in this chapter. Do any of these inhibit compliance in your company? If so, what actions might be needed?

20. Are there other non-value added GXP activities conducted in your company that do nothing to advance compliance? What actions are needed to eliminate these?

Chapter 8: Dear healthcare company: Do these things really benefit the patient?

21. Ask the following question of your organization: Have we forgotten our patient? Are we expending resources on activities that are not benefiting the patient (or anything else)? What are we doing that the patient (or anyone else, for that matter) would not pay extra for in product costs? Are there things we should cease doing?

22. How can we convey to our ultimate patients the value of the activities we are doing to improve their outcome?

Chapter 9: An FDA-483 observation is not necessarily the worst thing that can happen

23. Assess whether your company's handling of 483 observations includes, at a minimum, the items discussed in this chapter?

24. Discuss whether your actions to prevent a repeat 483 observation are adequate.

25. Determine what philosophical changes might be beneficial for your approach to and handling of 483 observations in this future.

Chapter 10: A contrarian's approach to GXP compliance and inspection readiness

26. Ask the contrarian's questions discussed in this chapter to, hopefully, identify new compliance vulnerabilities that should be addressed.

Chapter 11: Predictors of regulatory GXP inspection success: How do you know if you should worry about your next inspection?

27. Conduct a review of the "predictors of inspection success" discussed in this chapter. When viewed against your own operation, would you predict inspection success? If not, what actions might be warranted?

Chapter 12: Regulatory GXP inspections: trials, tribulations, and successes

28. Consider your own approach for which individuals interact with regulatory investigators on your site. Would this approach exude confidence in your personnel?

29. Review the management of your last regulatory inspection. Were documents provided quickly? Was the inspection organized? Was there adequate communication between functions? In short, what changes are needed before the next inspection? Should you conduct a dry-run to assess how changes will be implemented?

30. Ask how your team can stay better focused to the end of the next inspection? What actions are needed to remain motivated for an inspection that could last 3 weeks? 6 weeks? 6 months?

Chapter 13: Behind the scenes of a regulatory GXP inspection: Questions and Answers

31. Discuss what your team can do during the next regulatory inspection to enhance the relationship between your team and the inspection team?

32. Discuss what your team can do to enhance your relationship with key members of the FDA District Office management team (or other inspectorate management)?

Chapter 14: Things you should never say during a regulatory GXP inspection

33. Is your training for individuals that interact with regulatory investigators adequate? Does it include some training on what NOT to say?

34. What actions can you take now to better manage what is said across the organization during the next inspection?

Chapter 15: Actions you should take during those critical first 24 hours after closing a regulatory GXP inspection

35. Assess your post-inspection approach against the discussion and recommendations included in this chapter. What changes can you make to improve your own actions after the next regulatory inspection?

Chapter 16: Perspectives on healthcare from a patient's viewpoint

36. This chapter includes a discussion on the following:
    a. Risk/benefit assessment
    b. Outcome-based results
    c. Strongly integrated teamwork
    d. Continuous learning
    e. Embracing change
    f. Specialization versus generalization

    How can you use these emerging trends in healthcare to enhance your own approach to compliance? Are there areas in which you should be trending more toward these initiatives?

Chapter 17: What will inspections be like in the future?

37. Are your data accumulation, trend assessment, and progressive approach to compliance in line with future expectations regarding inspections? What steps are needed now to ready your operation for likely future inspection trends?

About the Author

Eldon Henson is a resident of Wentzville, Missouri, where he lives with his wife of 45 years. He is a father to three and grandfather to seven.

Eldon retired in 2016 after over 40 years working in the pharmaceutical industry where he was personally involved in over 100 regulatory inspections. Earlier in his career, he authored over 20 technical articles and was a frequent speaker at industry events, conferences, and seminars.

Later in his career, Eldon began a daily communication to employees in his company that provided encouragement, motivation, and inspiration on life and work. After he retired, Eldon began including much of this in a blog called "The Porch" at eldonhenson.com.

Eldon's first book, *"Achieving your best day yet!: A more fulfilling career… a more impactful life"*, is available through Amazon.

Eldon's email **henson333@hotmail.com**.